Television Production:
A Classroom Approach

Television Production:
A Classroom Approach

Second Edition

Student Edition

Keith Kyker and Christopher Curchy

LIBRARIES
UNLIMITED
A Member of the Greenwood Publishing Group

Westport, Connecticut • London

Library of Congress Cataloging-in-Publication Data

Kyker, Keith
    Television production : a classroom approach / Keith Kyker and Christopher
Curchy, 2nd ed.
      p. cm.
    Includes index.
    ISBN 1-59158-159-1 (student ed. : alk. paper)
    1. Television—Production and direction—Study and teaching. 2. Television—
Equipment and supplies. I. Kyker, Keith II. Curchy, Christopher
PN1992.75.K95 2004
791.4502'3'0711—dc22   2004048458

British Library Cataloguing in Publication Data is available.

Library of Congress Catalog Card Number: 2004048458
ISBN: 1-59158-159-1

First published in 2004

Libraries Unlimited, 88 Post Road West, Westport, CT 06881
A Member of the Greenwood Publishing Group, Inc.
www.lu.com

Printed in the United States of America

The paper used in this book complies with the
Permanent Paper Standard issued by the National
Information Standards Organization (Z39.48–1984).

10 9 8 7 6 5 4

CONTENTS

INTRODUCTION

Welcome to Television Production: A Classroom Approach

Why "A Classroom Approach?" Because if you're using this book, you're probably enrolled in a television production class. And classes are based on teaching and learning. There's a lot to learn if you're going to make good TV programs—programs that other people will want to watch.

Just about everybody likes TV. They might not be sure what they like about it or why they like it, but they like TV. This book is about making TV programs that people will like. That task is based on a clear knowledge of the basic skills of TV production and the ability to use those skills in carefully crafted projects.

You probably already know how to do several things: drive a car, play a musical instrument, hit a baseball, operate a computer program or video game. The first time you tried it, you knew what you *wanted* to do, but you probably weren't too successful. (Don't make us pull out the videos from the sixth-grade band concert!)

You had to learn the basics. After a while those basics became second nature, and you began to add your own personal style. Nobody wants to stay at the basic level very long. But if you don't learn the basics, nobody will want to watch your TV programs.

This book starts with the basics of camcorder operation and video shot composition. That's Chapter 1. Before you know it, you'll be using the "Rule of Thirds" to create the videography repertoire. Not sure what that means? Good. Wouldn't want you to get bored.

In Chapter 2, we'll look at microphones. Omnidirectional, unidirectional, PZM, shotgun—the list goes on. We'll also show you how to select the best microphone for each situation and how to use it properly. When you see a professional wrestler slam a microphone onto the floor, you'll want to call the cops. Trust us.

Chapter 3 continues the audio theme with a look at more equipment. We take a serious look at audio mixers and learn about different sources for music. You've probably heard about software that lets you make great-sounding music on your computer (even if you can't play a musical instrument). We hope you'll get the chance to try that soon.

In Chapter 4, we start thinking about extended video projects. A good project begins between the ears and then goes onto paper. You'll learn about scriptwriting and storyboarding, and you'll get a chance to make you own documentary.

Chapter 5 puts you on the scene to cover the news. If you're thinking about a career in broadcasting, working as a reporter or technician on a news-gathering team might just be your ticket to fame. News reporters travel all over the world and talk to some very interesting people. And they get paid to do this.

Chapter 6 looks at computer-based editing. A few years ago, editing at school meant you had to wait in line for an "editing suite" (that is, if you went to a school with the latest equipment), or use the 2-2-2 method (two VCRs, two TVs, and two fingers). Now video editing is done on computers. Your school might have stand-alone editing systems for you to use, or you might be editing on a customized desktop or laptop computer. Either way, it's a lot better than it used to be, and you can get as creative as you want.

In Chapter 7, we tackle studio production, including advanced video equipment, lighting, simple set design, and studio camera techniques. You'll also learn about the various studio crew positions on a television production team.

Everybody has a story to tell—a movie they'd like to make. Chapter 8 teaches the basics of movie production, including developing your ideas, writing a script, and shooting and editing your movie. This might be what attracted you to this class in the first place. Just remember us when you're making your speech at the Oscars.

Television production is your chance to show the world how you see the world. Our goal in this book is to teach you about the tools and techniques that let you make that happen.

There's a lot to learn. That's where the "classroom approach" comes in.

Keith Kyker and Christopher Curchy

2004

Objectives

After successfully completing this chapter, you will be able to

- identify the main parts of the camcorder and explain how they work together.
- identify various videotape formats and explain the advantages and disadvantages of each format.
- describe the operational controls and locate them on your camcorder.
- compose the shots in the videography repertoire.
- use a tripod to improve camcorder stability.
- create a videotaped program of still images using a camcorder and tripod.

Vocabulary

camcorder. An item of video equipment that uses a video camera permanently attached to a video deck to create and record video signal.

charge-coupled device (CCD). An imaging device used in most video cameras and camcorders.

focus. Adjustment made to the focal length of the lens to create a sharper, more defined picture.

lens. The curved glass on a video camera or camcorder that collects light.

tripod. A three-legged mounting device for a video camera or camcorder that provides stability.

videography. Operation of a video camera or camcorder in video production.

videography repertoire. A collection of six video shots that represents the standard work of videography. All videographers should learn to compose the shots in the videography repertoire properly.

videotape. A thin strip of plastic material containing metal particles that are capable of recording and storing a magnetic charge.

viewfinder and viewscreen. A small video monitor mounted on a video camera or camcorder that provides a view of the video image to the videographer. Viewfinders may be presented as eyepieces, as small screens mounted on the side of the camcorder, or as larger video monitors mounted near the top of a studio camera.

white balance. The process of adjusting the video camera or camcorder's color response to the surrounding light.

zoom lens. A lens with a variable focal length.

The camcorder is the workhorse of school television production—the most basic, and often the most advanced, item of equipment with which you'll make most of the projects in television production class. Almost every school video project involves picking up a camcorder and recording some video. In this chapter, we'll learn about the basic parts of the camcorder and how they work together to record audio and video. We'll also explore some of the basic operational controls of the camcorder, such as autofocus, automatic gain control, and white balance.

Because this book is all about using television production equipment to make video projects, we'll explore the videography repertoire. That's a fancy way of saying the shots you need to be able to create with your camcorder. We'll also learn several tips for adding a professional look to your videography. Finally, we'll learn about tripods, our trusty friends who always hold the camcorder steady and never complain.

The Camcorder: How It Works

When we learn about how the camcorder works, it's important to realize that a camcorder is actually two separate items of video production equipment—the video camera and the VCR (video cassette recorder). That's how the word "camcorder" was coined—a combination of "camera" and "recorder." In fact, in the early days of portable television production, the video camera and the VCR really were two pieces of equipment. The videographer (a person who operates a video camera or camcorder) would carry the video camera on his or her shoulder. The VCR—about the same size as the VCR you may have at home—was attached to a strap and carried on the shoulder, too. The two items were connected by a video cable, and often an audio (sound) cable, too. Early versions of this setup (camera and VCR) weighed 25 pounds or more, and even the later versions (around 1992) were still very heavy. Often school videographers would carry a tripod, and put the VCR on a media center cart. Operating a camcorder took not only skill, but muscles, too!

Now, of course, a high-quality camcorder fits in the palm of the hand (Figure 1.1). Even an elementary student can hold the combined video camera and VCR with no problem.

Even though the size of the equipment has changed over the years, the basic functions are still the same. In simplest terms, here's how a camcorder works: light, reflected off of an object, enters the camcorder lens. The lens focuses that light onto a light-sensing computer chip, called a CCD (charge-

Fig. 1.1. Videographers with camcorders.

coupled device). The CCD produces an electrical charge based on the amount of light that each tiny area of the CCD receives. That electrical video signal is recorded onto the videotape.

At the same time, the microphone mounted on the front of the camcorder detects minute changes in air pressure (sound waves) and converts those sound waves into electrical signal. That electrical audio signal is recorded on the videotape at the same time as the video signal.

As the signals are being recorded, they are instantly sent to a small video monitor (television) mounted on the camcorder, called a viewfinder or viewscreen. At the same time, the audio signal is sent to a headphone jack or a small speaker (or both). By using the viewfinder/viewscreen and headphones/speaker, videographers can see and hear what they are recording.

Okay, all that might seem a bit complicated. Here's an even shorter version. Light and sound enter the camcorder, are converted into electrical signals, and recorded onto a magnetic videotape. The signal is also sent to a tiny TV and speaker, so that videographers can see and hear what they are videotaping.

Now, let's look at each item in detail.

The Lens

A lens is a curved glass that focuses light onto a specific area (Figure 1.2). The camcorder lens accepts light from a wide vista and focuses it onto the CCD (light-sensing computer chip), which is about a half-inch wide.

Focus

Sometimes the videographer must make small changes in the length of the lens. This is called "focus." When you focus a lens, you are actually lengthening it, or shortening it. Focusing makes sure that a well-defined beam of light is projected onto the CCD. Almost all camcorders have automatic focus, discussed later in this chapter.

Fig. 1.2. A camcorder lens.

Iris

Inside the lens is a mechanism that allows the videographer to control the actual size of the lens opening. This control is called the iris. The lens opening is called the aperture. The iris controls the size of the aperture. Only rarely is the aperture 100 percent open. As you probably guessed, this would occur in a low-light situation, when the camcorder lens is trying to grab all of the light it can. But when operating in normal room light or daylight, the aperture is open only a fraction of its largest size. Most camcorders have automatic self-adjusting irises. You probably guessed this, because you've probably operated a camcorder at some point and probably never had to adjust the aperture by hand. Imagine you are videotaping a school play in an auditorium. Before the play begins, the lights dim, and your camcorder iris automatically adjusts the aperture to its largest setting. As the lights slowly illuminate the stage, the aperture becomes smaller and smaller.

Optical Zoom Lens

Almost all camcorders have an optical zoom lens. An optical zoom lens allows the videographer to create a close-up shot from a distance. (Some camcorders also have a digital zoom lens, which is explained later in this chapter.) An optical zoom lens has two extreme settings—telephoto and wide angle. The telephoto setting is the extreme close-up setting. The wide angle setting captures the largest view. Of course, the videographer can adjust the zoom lens anywhere in between the two extremes. This is known as "zooming-in" and "zooming-out." Typically, a camcorder's telephoto setting is 10 or 12 times normal vision, and its wide-angle setting is equivalent to normal vision. Therefore, the lens is indicated as 10 x 1, or 12 x 1.

Imaging Device

As we said earlier, the camcorder gathers light through the lens and converts that light into an electrical signal. That process is achieved by a computer chip called a "charge coupled device" (CCD; Figure 1.3). A CCD is about a half-inch across and is divided into hundreds of thousands of individual sections. Each section is capable of sensing light. The total video picture is created by the individual signals created by each of those sensing areas.

If each area can sense the presence and strength of light, how is a color video picture achieved? A striped filter is placed in front of the CCD that further divides the CCD into green, red, and blue sensing areas—some areas sense the color red, some sense the color blue, and others sense the color green.

Professional camcorders have three CCDs, not just one. In a 3-CCD camera, a prism splits the incoming light into the three primary colors of light (red, green, blue), and each color is processed by a dedicated CCD. A 3-CCD camera produces a very high-quality image because the picture is created using three times the number of sensing elements.

Fig. 1.3. A camcorder lens removed to reveal the charge-coupled device (CCD).

Recording onto Videotape

The electrical video signal is recorded onto videotape. Videotape is a thin strip of plastic, coated with metal particles. Those metal particles are magnetized by the electrical signal created by the CCD. As the videotape passes though the camcorder, the electrical signal is magnetically recorded. (A VCR can read that magnetic charge on the videotape.)

Videotape Formats

As video technology has evolved over the years, different, often smaller, videotape formats have evolved. Before camcorders were created, videotape recorders used two-inch-wide tape on open reels. Later, one-inch-wide open-reel tape was used—no videocassettes yet! The first videocassette contained three-quarter-inch-wide tape and was about twice the size of a regular VHS tape. The appearance of VHS (video home system) ushered in half-inch videotape. The smaller videocassette made the first camcorders possible. VHS camcorders (and SVHS, using the same sized videocassettes) were used extensively in schools in the late 1980s and 1990s. The last full-sized VHS camcorders were made in the late 1990s.

Now, several smaller-sized videocassette formats are used (Figure 1.4). Let's take a brief look at each one.

VHS-C. When most people think of a videocassette, they think of a VHS tape. Most home and classroom VCRs are VHS. When you rent a movie on videotape, you rent a VHS tape. If you go to the store and ask where the blank videotapes are located, they will probably point you to a rack of VHS tapes. For several years, almost all camcorders were VHS, too. With a videotape measuring about 7.5 inches long, however, VHS camcorders were large. The heavy camcorder was hoisted onto the shoulder of an adult (children weren't

Fig. 1.4. Videotape formats include VHS, VHS-C, 8mm, MiniDV.

strong enough), and videotape of the family picnic was made. The big benefit was that the VHS videotape could instantly be played using most home VCRs.

Of course, the big downside was the size. Taking a camcorder to Disneyland meant carrying around an extra piece of luggage. A smaller camcorder meant a smaller videotape. Thus, VHS-C was born. The "C" in VHS-C stands for "compact." A VHS-C videocassette is less than half the size of its full-size ancestor.

VHS-C camcorders are sometimes found in schools. Using an adapter, the VHS-C camcorder can be played in a VHS VCR. VHS-C camcorders are inexpensive, and tapes are moderately priced and readily available. The main disadvantage of the VHS-C camcorder is picture quality. Like VHS, the VHS-C videotape is capable of recording only 240 lines of resolution (less than half of higher-end formats mentioned later in this chapter). This low-quality acceptance means that VHS-C camcorders are designed for that family Disneyland trip. Often, VHS-C camcorders don't have the features that school videographers like to have.

SVHS-C. When full-sized VHS was the king of the camcorder world, some videographers really wanted a higher-quality picture. SVHS (Super VHS) was developed for this audience. Blank SVHS videotapes look just like VHS tapes, but the higher-quality videotape allows for recording of the SVHS signal (about 400 lines of resolution). SVHS isn't just high-quality VHS—the signal is truly different and incompatible with VHS.

SVHS-C videocassettes appeared about the same time as VHS-C. The smaller videocassette means a smaller camcorder. The high-quality signal is attractive to more serious videographers, and SVHS-C camcorders often have advanced features. Unfortunately, to truly realize the SVHS-C picture quality, you must play the SVHS-C videocassette using an SVHS VCR, and most people don't buy those.

The 8mm formats. About the time that VHS-C camcorders appeared, two new formats hit the market that are totally incompatible with the VHS equipment found in most homes and schools. These two formats were 8mm (eight millimeter) and Hi8mm (high eight millimeter). Both of these formats use a very small videocassette packed with 8mm-wide videotape. The picture quality of 8mm is comparable to VHS-C, and Hi8mm is similar to SVHS-C. The problem, of course, is that almost no one owns an 8mm VCR, and no adapter will make the 8mm videocassette fit into the VHS VCR. Most 8mm camcorder users have to connect their camcorders to VCRs and TVs to record and watch their programs.

Digital Video Formats. The two newest videotape formats—Mini DV and DV8mm offer astounding picture quality with a small camcorder at a reasonable price. Mini DV and DV8mm millimeter camcorders record a true digital signal (computer code—0s and 1s) onto a magnetic videotape. This is actually very similar to copying a file onto a floppy diskette. The audio and video, recorded as digital information on the videotape, produces 480 lines of resolution (twice the quality of VHS) and sound that rivals a compact disc. Probably the most unique feature of a digital camcorder is the computer connector known as IEEE-1394. This type of connector is known as "FireWire" (Apple Computer™) and "i.LINK" (Sony™). When the IEEE-1394 connector is attached to a computer or nonlinear editing system, you can download your footage directly as a computer file. (Nonlinear editing is discussed in Chapter 6.)

MiniDV is becoming the format of choice for videographers, and DV8mm is losing popularity. MiniDV VCRs are now available, and MiniDV camcorders are available in inexpensive models designed for the family and professional 3-CCD camcorders as well.

So to summarize the format choices:

	Advantages	**Disadvantages**
VHS-C	Small camcorder size	Average picture quality; adapter required for playback; no digital connection
S-VHS-C	Better picture quality; small camcorder size	Adapter required for playback; no digital connection
Hi-8 and 8mm	Good picture quality; small camcorder size	Not compatible with most school VCRs; no digital connection
Digital formats (MiniDV and DV8mm)	Outstanding picture and sound quality; IEEE-1394 connector (compatible with nonlinear editing devices); small camcorder size	None

Non-Videotape Formats

If you think about it, it is rather odd to record a digital video signal on a videotape. It reminds us of those old computers in the 1960s and 1970s that recorded data on giant open reels of computer tape. It makes more sense to record the video and audio signals onto a format that you can instantly insert into your computer.

Camcorders that record onto DVD-R and DVD-RAM discs are now available and will soon become established camcorder choices. The DVD-RAM discs can be erased and reused. The DVD-R discs are single use; you cannot erase and reuse a DVD-R. DVDs created using these camcorders hold about two hours of video and can be played in home DVD players and used in nonlinear editing systems with DVD drives. Videographers who use DVD-R and DVD-RAM camcorders don't have to connect their camcorders to their nonlinear editing system to import footage. They can simply place the recorded DVD in their computer's DVD drive. (Nonlinear editing systems are described in Chapter 6.)

Camcorders that record directly onto internal hard drives are also appearing on the market. Computer hard drives are getting smaller and faster. It makes sense to install one of those hard drives in a camcorder and record the digital signal directly onto that hard drive. The limitation now is the size of the hard drive. The camcorder can only record a few hours of footage. When the camcorder's hard drive is full, it must be dumped into the computer, then erased. As hard drive space increases to the terabyte level in years to come, however, expect hard-drive-based camcorders to make a big impact.

The Microphone

So far, we've been talking mostly about video. All camcorders also have microphones to collect sound. Typically, the microphone is mounted on the front of the camcorder. Some camcorders have two microphones, allowing for stereo recording. These microphones are so close together, however, that a real stereo (two-channel) effect is never achieved. Most videographers will want to connect an external microphone to their camcorder to collect more specific sounds. In fact, these microphones are so important that they get their own chapter—Chapter 2.

Headphones and Speakers

Most videographers will want to hear the audio as it is being recorded. For this reason, a headphone jack is a must on all school camcorders. Imagine interviewing the principal only to realize when you get back to the classroom that your microphone wasn't turned on. Some camcorders also have small speakers, so that you can hear the sound recorded on the videotape when it is played using the camcorder.

The Viewfinder and Viewscreen

The viewfinder is the tiny video monitor mounted near the top of the camcorder. Videographers place their eye against a rubber pad next to the viewfinder to see what they are recording—what the camera "is seeing" (Figure 1.5). Sometimes the term "EVF" is used for "electronic viewfinder." Believe it or not, in the early days of portable video production some camcorders had "optical viewfinders." An optical viewfinder was a small plastic circle on the camcorder. Videographers would point the camcorder and look through the circle to get an estimation of what they were recording, much like a hunter aiming down the barrel of a gun. Can you imagine trying to create good video shots without the benefit of an electronic viewfinder?

When camcorders were larger, they were almost always held with the weight of the camcorder on the right shoulder. Naturally, the electronic viewfinder was mounted on the left side of the camcorder, for easy access by the videographer. Now that camcorders are smaller and can be held in the palm of the hand, the viewfinder is typically mounted at the top of the camcorder near the center.

Of course, the smaller camcorders have also allowed for the popular viewscreen. The viewscreen is a small (usually about three inches) color monitor that typically flips out from the side of the camcorder (Figure 1.6). Using the viewscreen, videographers can operate the camcorder and create great shots without having the camcorder pressed against their face. Most viewscreens also swivel and tilt, allowing operation

Fig. 1.5. A videographer using a camcorder viewfinder.

from a variety of angles. The viewscreen also allows for easy, convenient viewing of recorded videotape. A small, built-in speaker or headphone set can provide the audio.

Operational Controls

Now that you've learned about the basic parts and features of the camcorder, let's look at the camcorder's operational controls—in other words, those little buttons that control the way the camcorder is operated (Figure 1.7).

Fig. 1.6. A camcorder viewscreen.

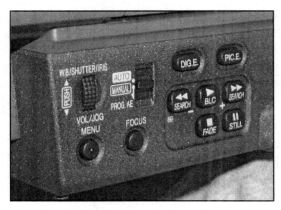

Fig. 1.7. Camcorder controls.

If possible, it would be a good idea to have your camcorder (or a few pages from the owner's manual) nearby as you read this section. Different camcorder models have different features. Some camcorders will have all of the controls listed here, while less-developed models will have only a few. You might have to access some of these controls by scrolling through menus on the viewscreen. Others will be accessible using buttons and dials on the camcorder.

The Power Switch

The first operational control is so basic, you might even think it's not worth reading about it. But you'd be surprised at how many beginning videographers leave the classroom without knowing how to turn the camcorder on! Your camcorder's power switch is probably a three-way switch: off, camera, and VCR. Of course, the camcorder is receiving no power in the "off" position. When the switch is in the "camera" position, the camcorder is ready to record videotape. In the VCR position, the videographer can use the camcorder to play a videotape.

Battery Release

Most of the time, you will use battery power for your camcorder. With some camcorders, you slide the battery in a small trapdoor and then securely close the door. With most camcorders, the battery slides into a little locking mechanism on the back of the camcorder. The battery clicks into place, and the battery release switch is used to remove the battery. Whether you have an internal or external battery connection, make sure you know how to remove the camcorder battery and install a new one.

Recording Start and Stop

The camcorder will have at least one button (usually red) that, when pressed, will start and stop the recording of signals onto the tape. Typically, the button is placed near the spot where the videographer's thumb normally rests. Sometimes an additional start/stop button is placed on the camcorder. Pressing the button once starts the recording, and pressing it again pauses the videotape. One thing to remember—it usually takes a second or two for tape to start rolling once the start/stop button is pressed. Make sure your on-camera talent doesn't start talking as soon as you press the start/stop button. If so, you will miss the first few seconds of her introduction.

Zoom Lens Control

Earlier in this chapter, we discussed the zoom lens that lets you get close-ups of distant objects. That zoom-in and zoom-out function is controlled by two buttons on the camcorder. For convenience, these buttons are usually mounted near where the videographer's middle and index finger would normally rest. These buttons are labeled "T" for telephoto (zoom in) and "W" for wide angle (zoom out). The T button is often mounted closer to the front of the camera, and the W button is right behind it. That way, you remember that when you press the button toward the subject, the shot will become a close-up. On some camcorders, the buttons are side by side. Examine your camcorder and learn how to zoom in and out.

Digital Zoom

When we looked at your camcorder's zoom lens earlier in this chapter, we used terms such as 10 x 1 and 12 x 1 to indicate the strength of the lens. Your camcorder is probably capable of much stronger zooms, however—100 x 1, 200 x 1, and even 300 x 1. This is made possible by your camcorder's digital zoom control. When you operate the optical zoom lens to zoom in and zoom out, you are actually controlling the length of the lens. As the optical zoom gets stronger, the lens gets longer inside its housing. To get a 200 x 1 optical zoom, you'd need an exceptionally long lens, like the lenses used by sideline photographers at football games. Obviously, your camcorder doesn't have a lens that long. Instead, the camcorder uses digital zoom technology. The image is trimmed both vertically and horizontally, and the smaller, trimmed image is enlarged to full frame.

Early versions of digital zoom produced grainy images. The picture wasn't very sharp to begin with, and as it was trimmed and enlarged, the picture quality suffered. Camcorders made during the last few years can produce a fairly high-quality digital zoom, however.

Accessing your camcorder's digital zoom function might require pushing a button, or making a choice on a menu screen. Typically, after that choice is made, the zoom control (telephoto and wide buttons) takes over the digital zoom function as well. As you zoom in, the camcorder stays with the optical zoom until it reaches its maximum setting—usually 10 x 1 or 12 x 1. After that, the digital zoom automatically engages. As you continue to press the "T" button (telephoto), the digital zoom continues to trim and magnify the shot.

Manual and Automatic Focus

You focus your camcorder to make the video clear, not blurry. Almost all camcorders have autofocus, which allows the camcorder to focus itself. (Usually, this is achieved as the camcorder sends out an invisible light beam and times how long it takes for the beam to bounce off the subject and return.)

Autofocus is generally a very useful feature, but it is also nice to be able to turn it off. Imagine you are videotaping your school's homecoming parade. You are standing on a platform, using a tripod. You videotape the floats, bands, and cars as they parade by. Occasionally, however, a fellow student briefly walks in front of the camera. On autofocus, the camcorder would immediately focus on that student and then take a few seconds to focus back on the parade. In this case, manual focus would be a better selection.

If your camcorder has manual focus, you need to learn two things: how to switch between autofocus and manual focus, and how to focus the camera in the manual mode to create a sharp picture. Usually, a button switches the camcorder from auto to manual focus, and back again. Often a dial is used to focus the camera manually. Your camcorder owner's manual is the best resource for determining these controls.

Fade

The camcorder's fade control slowly fades your video to black, or to another color you can select. Usually the audio fades in and out at the same time. By holding in the fade button, the camcorder goes to black/silent. When you release the button, the picture slowly appears, and the audio reaches the correct level.

Fade is a useful function when you are videotaping a program that will not be edited. For example, if you are videotaping a guest speaker, you might want to fade in as the speaker is introduced, and fade out at the conclusion of her speech. Or, if you are videotaping a piano recital, you might want to fade out at the conclusion of each selection, pause the camcorder, then unpause and fade in as the next pianist is introduced. If you are using a nonlinear (computer-based) editing system, then you probably won't use the fade control very much. It will be just as easy to add your fades in the editing process.

White Balance

White balance is the adjustment on you camera that determines how the camera processes colors. Even though we don't think about it, light has a distinct tint, and that colorization shows up on video. Programs shot under fluorescent light can look blue, and programs shot under regular light bulbs can have a reddish tint. The white balance control allows the camera to compensate for such unwanted tints in our video.

There are many types of white balance, depending on the sophistication of your camcorder. All camcorders have automatic white balance that do an average job of compensating for lighting differences. Almost all camcorders have preset settings. Usually these are represented by small icons on the viewfinder, such as a sun, a light bulb, and so on. These settings, set by the videographer, are almost always superior to the automatic setting.

Other camcorders have manual white balance controls that give a truer setting. Usually, the videographer presses a white balance button and shows the camcorder something white—a blank note card, for example. The camcorder then adjusts the colors based on that white sample. Of course, when the lighting changes—when the videographer goes outside, for example—then he must white balance again under the new lighting situation. Whether your camcorder allows you to adjust for specific lighting environments or simply select between "indoor" and "outdoor" settings, make sure to white balance every time you videotape a project.

Automatic Gain Control (AGC)

Some camcorders have a function called automatic gain control, or AGC for short. AGC adjusts the camcorder video signal to create the best shots. If the video is too bright, the AGC will decrease the electrical signal. If the shot is dim, AGC will boost the signal. Don't confuse this with the automatic iris listed earlier in this chapter. The iris actually controls the amount of light hitting the CCD. The AGC control adjusts the signal that is recorded on the videotape.

Electronic Image Stabilization (EIS)

Ever since camcorders were small enough to hold in the hand or on the shoulder, videographers have looked for ways to create steady shots. Tripods are great, but we don't always have the time or the space. Electronic Image Stabilization—EIS—is a high-tech solution available on many camcorders. EIS is actually a complex electronic process. Each image that the camcorder produces is electronically analyzed and compared with the image just before it, especially around the edges. EIS corrects minor changes instantaneously, before the image is recorded onto videotape. This happens 30 times every second! Although EIS doesn't solve extreme camera shaking, it does help with minor movements caused by breathing (popular with all videographers!) and small hand movements.

High-speed Shutter

Do you have experience with "regular" print photography? If so, you understand the concept of shutter speed. The photographer can adjust the shutter speed on her camera to capture fast-moving objects, such as a swinging baseball bat or a butterfly fluttering by. Without high-speed shutter, the picture would just be a blur.

Of course, camcorders don't have shutters. The camcorder lens is always open (unless a lens cap covers it). So a camcorder's high-speed shutter really isn't a shutter function at all—that would be impossible. The feature is called high-speed shutter because most people can relate to the need to capture quickly moving images, and that's just what the camcorder's high-speed shutter does.

Instead of adjusting a nonexistent shutter, the camcorder's shutter speed function actually divides the CCD into sections, allowing it to create more individual images than normal. This allows the videographer to recorded subjects that move at high speeds with more clarity and also provides sharper paused images. An example would be a model-rocket liftoff in science class. As the rocket zips off the launch pad, the camcorder without the high-speed shutter setting would probably record only a puff of smoke. The high-speed shutter would allow the teacher to pause the videotape during playback and show the class a still-frame of the moment of launch.

Graphics

Most camcorders have built-in graphics. At the touch of a button, the words "Happy Birthday" can appear on the screen. Some camcorders can put the date and time on the screen (and the date is almost always wrong!). These onscreen graphics might be fun for the video hobbyist but are probably not useful in the school production setting. Why do we mention them? Because you need to know how to turn them *off!*

Recognize when you have accidentally activated those graphics and quickly remove them from your viewfinder. How embarrassed would you be if the entire football game was videotaped with the caption "A Special Day" over every play?

Videotape Playback Controls

Usually we think of the camcorder doing what it was built to do—recording videotape. But your camcorder is also a VCR and can play videotapes. Although even the comparatively large viewscreen is small, you can use it to watch the videotape that you just shot to make sure that you "got it!" (You can also use headphones to listen to the videotape. Some camcorders have built-in speakers as well.)

Playback controls that you can expect to find on your camcorder include PLAY, PAUSE, STOP, FAST FORWARD, and REWIND.

Some camcorders have an additional playback control called RECORD REVIEW. When this button is pressed, the videotape rewinds a couple of seconds and plays that last little bit of videotape. The benefit is to allow the videographer to determine the quality or topic of the last scene recorded. Record review can usually be accessed while the camcorder is still on the RECORD setting. (The other controls require the camcorder to be switched to the VCR setting.)

Inputs and Outputs

Camcorders usually have inputs and outputs that enable the connection to other items of equipment (Figure 1.8). The most typical input is a microphone jack. (We'll discuss microphones in detail in Chapter 2.) You will probably want to plug in a microphone for almost every video project. Some camcorders, especially the digital formats, also have audio and video inputs. This allows the user to connect a nondigital video format (such as a VHS VCR) to the camcorder, and use the camcorder to record a MiniDV tape. Then that MiniDV tape can be imported into a computer for nonlinear editing.

Audio and video outputs are important when we use our camcorders as part of a small studio setup or as equipment to edit videotape. Composite audio and video jacks can be connected to a VHS VCR to make a videotape that can be played in the VHS VCRs in millions of American homes. An S-VHS output would be useful when connecting the camcorder to a video mixer or character generator. Of course, the IEEE-1394 connector— known as i.Link or FireWire—sends both the audio and video signals to a computer for editing. The same connection receives the signals for recording back onto the digital videotape. (Because the IEEE-1394 connector carries a digital signal, it is typically found only on digital camcorders.) As mentioned earlier, a headphone jack is also an important output.

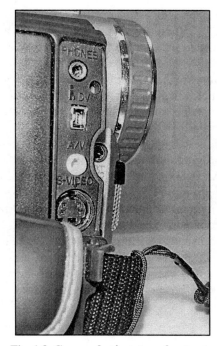

Don't worry if you're not sure about all of those inputs and outputs. We'll explore them later in this course. Just understand that most camcorders were designed to function with other items of video and audio production, and these inputs and outputs make it possible.

Fig. 1.8. Camcorder inputs and outputs.

Videography Basics

Now that we've learned how the camcorder works, let's explore how we can use the camcorder to make some great programs! You need to become a videographer!

A videographer is someone who uses a video camera or camcorder to create professional-looking television programs. This is more than just a camera operator. Videography involves skill, knowledge of standard shots, patience, and practice. Some students will pick up the skills of videography quickly. Others need more practice. But it's important for everyone in class to learn the basics.

In this section, we'll discuss two topics that will get you well on your way: creating the shots in the videography repertoire and tips to make your video shots look professional—like the work of a videographer!

The Videography Repertoire

Whether you're working on a school video project or network television program, you need to know how to create some basic video production shots. This collection of shots is called the videography repertoire. Maybe you've been a part of a musical group (a band, a choir) that could perform several songs. This collection of songs was your group's repertoire. Videographers have a repertoire that consists of six shots that are standards in video production. When you learn to create and recognize these shots, you'll be ready to plan and shoot your video project.

Long Shot

A long shot contains the entire subject that you are shooting (Figure 1.9). For example, a long shot of a person would include the person from head to toe. A long shot of a house would include the entire house. A long shot of a professional football stadium would probably be taken from an airplane or blimp. You get the idea—a long shot has it all.

When creating a long shot of a person, make sure to include the feet, and a small amount of space below the feet. Don't cut off the top of the head. It is important for all of your long shots of people to include headroom—a small but comfortable amount of space between the top of the person's head and the top of the screen.

A long shot of a building or park where the video program will take place is called an establishing shot. An establishing shot often appears at the beginning of a program. For example, a long shot of a school could begin an orientation video. It would immediately let your audience know the subject of your video. Of course, establishing shots can also be used to trick the viewer. An establishing shot of a hospital instantly implies the setting. The rest of the video, however, could be shot on a television studio set.

Fig. 1.9. Long shot.

Medium Shot 2

A medium shot usually describes a person. The shot includes the body from the knee area and up (Figure 1.10). Medium shots are frequently used by videographers videotaping a news reporter on location.

Here's an important concept when creating any shot involving a person: never put a natural body line at the bottom of the screen. Natural body lines include the ankles, the knees, the waist, the bust line, and the neck. Putting one of those lines at the bottom of the screen makes the shot look eerily awkward—like the person doesn't have a body below that point. So, when creating a medium shot, make sure to place the area just above the knees, or just below the knees at the bottom of the screen. Both versions correctly describe the medium shot.

Fig. 1.10. Medium shot.

Bust Shot 3

The bust shot includes the head and shoulders of the person (Figure 1.11). If you went to a museum, you might see head-and-shoulder statues of famous people. These statues are called busts. As with the long shot and medium shot, make sure to include a small but comfortable amount of headroom when creating your bust shots. A school picture in a yearbook is a good example of a bust shot.

Close-up 4

A close-up of a person includes his or her head and neck (Figure 1.12). The amount of headroom in a close-up may be very small. (If the subject has a full hairstyle, there may be no visible headroom.) Because they are similar, beginning videographers often confuse the bust shot with the close-up. Here's a good rule to remember: the bust shot includes the curve of the shoulders; the close-up does not.

A close-up can also describe a shot of a certain part of a larger subject. For example, imagine you are videotaping a science experiment. A beaker of liquid is heating atop a Bunsen burner. The science teacher might ask you to "get a close-up" of the liquid as she adds another ingredient to the liquid.

Fig. 1.11. Bust shot.

Fig. 1.12. Close-up.

Also, if you are working as part of a video crew, realize that your director may ask you to make small adjustments in your shots. For example, the director might say "tighten-up that close-up." This means that you should get a little closer to your subject and fill the screen a little more.

Extreme Close-up 5

As the name implies, an extreme close-up is even closer than a close-up. An extreme close-up of a person would include only part of the person's face (Figure 1.13). For example, an extreme close-up could capture concentration in your subject's eyes as he struggles to solve a math problem. An extreme close-up is a great way to show emotional responses in your subjects.

Fig. 1.13. Extreme close-up.

Over-the-Shoulder Shot 6

Here's another descriptive name. To create the over-the-shoulder shot, the videographer positions himself behind the subject at an angle. This allows the audience to peak over the subject's shoulder and observe what she is doing (Figure 1.14). The over-the-shoulder shot is a great way to bring your audience into the action.

Those are the six basic shots that make up the videography repertoire. Practice with your camcorder and become an expert.

Videography Tips

Even after you've mastered the videography repertoire, you'll still need to master your videography skills. Here are some important tips for excellent videography.

Fig. 1.14. Over-the-shoulder shot.

Fill the Screen

Determine the true subject of your shot and fill the screen with that subject. Beginning videographers often include too much extra scenery. They don't get close enough to their subjects. Filling the screen with your subject will focus your audience's attention on the concept you're trying to communicate.

Provide Detail

Along the same line, use close-up shots to provide the correct amount of detail to your shots. Imagine you're creating a video about checking a car's tire pressure. When it's time to determine the air pressure, make sure to take your audience close enough to read the numbers on the tire gauge.

Create Your Shot, Then Record

Earlier in this chapter, we discussed the videography repertoire and the importance of creating good shots. When videotaping, it is important to create the shot before recording. Excessive cameras movements will make your videos look like home movies. Even if you're looking for a modern, moving camera style of videography, plan your shots before your press the record button. This will save time in the editing process and will make watching your footage a pleasant experience.

Roll Plenty of Videotape

Make sure that you roll plenty of videotape before the action begins and after the action has concluded. Camcorders require one or two seconds to start up once the record button is pressed. Try that with your camcorder. Begin counting aloud at the precise moment that you roll videotape. Then play the tape and listen. When did the camcorder actually start recording? You probably counted to "one" or "two" before the camcorder engaged. Also, make sure you roll videotape for a few seconds after the action has concluded. This way, you'll make sure to get all of the action. Some camcorders actually roll back one second after each shot. If you're not careful, you could lose the end of your interview or dramatic sequence.

Walk, Don't Zoom

Want to fill the screen with a shot of students studying in the library or get a close-up of the water fountain nozzle? Zoom out all the way and walk to the shot, instead of zooming in. Lazy camera operators will simply stand in one place and zoom in on each subject of their program. (This reminds us of the spoiled baby who points and cries for a cookie.) You will find that your camera shots are much clearer and less shaky when you walk close to create the shot instead of zooming in from across the room. Also, the autofocus will work much more quickly when the camera is close to the subject. Don't be a "me cookie" videographer. Walk to the shot before pressing the record button.

Find the Proper Level for Your Shot

Most camera angles are much more pleasing when the camera is on the same level as the person or item you are videotaping (Figures 1.15 and 1.16). This is especially important if you have the opportunity to videotape little children (like a preschool class coloring art projects). It would be easier for you to just stand over them, but that camera angle wouldn't capture the children's facial expressions. Examine each shot—if you're taller, you might find yourself "taking a knee" sometimes.

Fig. 1.15. Improper level (too high).

Fig. 1.16. Correct level.

Beware of Backlighting 8 (good / bad)

Earlier in this chapter, we explained that camcorders have an automatic iris function. The iris automatically increases and decreases, depending on the amount of light in the shot. But what happens when your subject (maybe someone conducting an on-camera interview) is standing in front of a sunny window? The iris becomes very small to accommodate the bright sunlight, and your interviewer looks like a silhouette (Figure 1.17). The camera doesn't know that the reporter is more important than the bright background—it's just adjusting to the light. That's why you always have to make sure that your subject is the brightest part of your shot. In this case, you might have to reposition the reporter so that she is standing in the daylight, or the background is less bright (Figure 1.18). You might also have access to a light for your camcorder. A less desirable option is to use the camcorder's backlight or AGC button. This would brighten your subject, but your background would be washed out. The best option is to plan your shots carefully and use a light if absolutely necessary.

Fig. 1.17. Backlighting leaves the subject in silhouette.

Fig. 1.18. Corrected shot: the subject is the brightest part of the shot.

Trust the Viewfinder

Whether you're using a viewfinder with an eyepiece or a flip-out viewscreen, be aware that you will see a fairly accurate representation of what you are recording on videotape. In other words, what you see is what you get! If it looks bad in the viewfinder, then it will look bad when you play the tape in the classroom or studio. Also, learn the symbols that your camcorder displays in the viewfinder. Modern camcorders have many functions and controls. Know what to look for in your viewfinder or viewscreen.

Use the Appropriate Amount of Headroom 9 (good / bad)

When videotaping people, make sure that you have a small but comfortable amount of space between the top of the head and the top of the screen (Figures 1.19 and 1.20). This is a difficult concept to explain in a book. The best way to learn the appropriate amount of headroom is to watch the work of advanced videographers. (Watch local and network news stories—they are a great source of professional live-action videography.)

Fig. 1.19. Too much headroom.

Fig. 1.20. Appropriate amount of headroom.

Use the Rule of Thirds 10

When creating a camera shot, divide the screen into thirds, both vertically and horizontally (Figure 1.21). In other words, draw an imaginary tic-tac-toe grid on the screen. The Rule of Thirds states that the most interesting parts of your shot should be on the "thirds." This goes against the classic "centering" technique, in which the subject is always smack-dab in the middle of the screen. The Rule of Thirds makes your shots interesting and dynamic.

Leadroom 11

Leadroom is a concept similar to headroom. When a subject is in profile or is walking from one side of the screen to the other, you need to create the shot so that he has most of the screen in front of him (Figure 1.22). Your audience needs to be able to see what the subject is looking at or approaching. Imagine you are videotaping a person as a long shot, and she is walking across a parking lot, from left to right. You need to keep the subject on the left "third," as described in the Rule of Thirds section. So about two-thirds of the shot shows the audience the area the person is approaching. A skilled videographer can pan the camera from left to right as the person walks, keeping her on the left-most third.

Fig. 1.21. Rule of Thirds: placing your subject on the "third" improves shot composition.

Fig. 1.22. Appropriate amount of leadroom.

Create Depth (Foreground, Middle Ground, Background)

A video screen is two-dimensional. It has height and width, but not depth. In other words, it is flat. Your challenge as a videographer is to create depth in your shots. How can you do this? The best way to create an illusion of depth is to make sure all of your shots have foreground (something in the front), middle ground (something in the middle—usually your subject), and background. Look at two examples: the first features our reporter against a brick wall—no depth there (Figure 1.23). The second example has a great deal of depth (Figure 1.24). There's foreground (the reporter), middle ground (the trees and shrubs), and background (the school building). You might want to think of these shots as postcard or magazine cover shots. Professional photographers and videographers use this technique to create shots that pull the viewer into the scene. You can, too.

Fig. 1.23. Shot with no depth.

Act Professionally

Videography is an attitude. A good videographer exudes confidence because they know how to create the shots of video production effectively. Your subjects—whether they are professional reporters or inexperienced participants—will pick up on the attitude you are projecting. If you are visibly nervous about creating the shots, your subjects won't feel too confident (no one wants to look bad on camera). Approach an assignment with professionalism. Sure, you can have fun with it. Just make sure to create an atmosphere that builds confidence in your group.

Fig. 1.24. Shot created with depth.

Use a Tripod When You Need It

A good videographer knows when he or she needs a little help. A tripod is a true friend. A tripod will hold your camera for hours, never shake or wiggle, and never complain. Of course, you don't need a tripod for every shot. Those one-minute interviews, the man-on-the-street reactions, and the random shots around school don't require a tripod. These shots are brief, and most videographers can hold the camera steady for that amount of time. Also, sometimes tripods just aren't practical. If you're standing on the sideline at a football game, you certainly won't have time to set up your tripod every time the ball moves down the field. But for those times that a steady shot is required and the production will last more than a minute or two, a tripod is required equipment. A drama production, a band concert, a dance recital—all of these are examples of situations that require tripods.

Tripods

This brings us to the final part of this lengthy introductory chapter—the tripod. In the previous paragraphs, we mentioned some situations in which a tripod would be useful. Now let's take a look at this loyal friend (Figure 1.25).

A tripod can be divided into two parts: the tripod and the tripod head. Usually when we think of a tripod, we think of the entire device, but the bottom part of the tripod—the three legs and the supporting braces—is known as the tripod base. The top-most part that the videographer uses to move the camera back and forth, left and right, is known as the tripod head.

This difference is especially important if you ever have the chance to buy a tripod. Many tripods are purchased in two pieces—the tripod base, and the tripod head. The purchaser needs to make sure he is buying both pieces.

Fig. 1.25. A tripod provides steady, tireless service.

There are various models of tripod bases to choose from. Some have thick, tubular legs, and others are made of thinner material. Some tripods can be adjusted to become very tall or very small; others only have a small range of adjustment. The main thing to consider about the tripod base is whether it is strong enough to hold your camcorder. Most tripods have recommended weight limits. Exceeding those limits might bring your production to a crashing end!

Tripod heads also vary in the marketplace. Some are "fluid heads." In this case, the tripod head is actually filled with a thick fluid that makes smooth camera movement much easier. Most tripod heads feature screws that are loosened to allow camera movement and then tightened to secure the camera in place. Some tripods have small bubble levels to allow the videographer to check the balance of the tripod.

The connection of the camcorder to the tripod is very important. A screw on the tripod head fits into a hole in the bottom of the camcorder. (This hole is the same size on every camcorder and tripod, so you don't have to worry about getting the right size screw on your tripod head.) A more convenient way to connect the camcorder to the tripod head is the quick-release system (Figure 1.26). A tripod head featuring the quick-release system has a detachable plate that screws into the bottom of the camcorder. That plate latches into the top of the tripod head and is secured by a convenient lever. Attaching the camcorder to the tripod head is quick and convenient.

Tripod Camcorder Movements

A tripod would be a great item to have if it only performed its primary task—holding the camcorder. However, the tripod—or more correctly the tripod head—can also help with camera movements. These movements include pan, tilt, truck, dolly, raising, and lowering.

Fig. 1.26. The quick-release system.

Pan

A pan is a side-to-side (for example, left to right) movement of the camcorder. Sure, you can pan without the tripod—just holding the camcorder. But a tripod helps you perform a smooth, level pan. A television director would say to the camera operator, "pan left" or "pan right" to indicate this movement.

Tilt

A tilt is a vertical (top to bottom or bottom to top) movement of the camcorder on the tripod. Starting at the front door and tilting all the way to the top of a skyscraper can dramatize the height of the building. The tripod head provides a firm centering point for the tilt movement. The director's command would be "tilt up" or "tilt down."

Truck and Dolly

The next two tripod camcorder movements, truck and dolly, require a tripod dolly to be attached to the bottom of the tripod. The tripod dolly is a set of wheels or casters on a frame that attaches to the bottom of the tripod legs. In the early days of television production, dollies were important because the television cameras were too large to move without wheels. Today the main function for the dolly is to enable camera movement that contributes to the production.

That said, the truck is a sideways movement of the tripod dolly. The director would instruct the camera operator to "truck left" or "truck right." The dolly is a forward or backward movement of the tripod dolly. The director's instruction would be "dolly in" or "dolly out."

Raising and Lowering the Tripod

Most tripods have a crank with a small teeth-and-gear mechanism. The camera operator can raise and lower the tripod using this crank. Very expensive tripods have smooth cranking operations. A skilled camera operator might be able to raise and lower this tripod slowly while the shot is rolling. Raising and lowering of most tripods is done when the camera is not recording. A director would probably instruct the camera operator to "raise" or "lower" the camcorder, although the terms "crank-up" and "crank-down" are also used.

The Mini-Tripod and the Monopod—Two Additional Camcorder Supports

Two other commonly used camcorder supports are worth mentioning—the mini-tripod and the monopod.

Mini-Tripod

A mini-tripod is a very small tripod—less than a foot tall (Figure 1.27). Mini-tripods are designed to be used with small cameras and camcorders. The mini-tripod can be used on a desktop or a conference table. Most mini-tripods are very simple —just three tubular aluminum legs with a screw on top (no fancy tripod head). Sometimes the legs expand to give more height. Rubber leg-tips keep the mini-tripod from sliding across the tabletop. Mini-tripods are very reasonably priced— often less than 10 dollars. A mini-tripod can make a great addition to the camcorder bag.

Fig. 1.27. The mini-tripod is suitable for tabletop use with small camcorders.

Monopod

Imagine a tripod with just one leg. That's a monopod (Figure 1.28). So how does the monopod defy the laws of gravity and balance the camcorder on just one leg? It doesn't. The videographer must provide the balance needed. The monopod provides the support.

When camcorders were very heavy, the monopod was an important tool for news and sports videography. Now, with lighter camcorders available, monopods are less common. Still, when videotaping a volleyball game or a press conference, you might find your arm and wrist getting tired. A monopod would be a big help.

This first chapter has covered a great deal of information about using a camcorder. Remember—good camera work takes practice. Written lessons are important, but the best way to learn videography skills is to grab a camcorder and make some tape!

Fig. 1.28. The monopod bears the camera weight and is easier to maneuver than the tripod.

Selected Manufacturer Web Sites

Bogen Manfrotto (tripods, monopods) http://www.bogenphoto.com
Davis & Sanford (tripods, monopods) http://www.tiffen.com/tripod_page.htm
JVC (camcorders, video equipment) http://www.jvc.com
Panasonic (camcorders, video equipment) http://www.panasonic.com
Sima (tripods, monopods, mini-tripods) http://www.simacorp.com
Sony (camcorders, video equipment) http://www.sonystyle.com

Review Questions

1. Briefly explain how the lens and the CCD work together to produce a video signal.

2. List four videotape formats currently being used and each format's advantages and disadvantages.

3. List three non-videotape formats for recording. Why would these formats be attractive to camcorder users?

4. A zoom lens control is typically labeled "T" and "W." What do those two letters mean, and what happens when each button is pressed?

5. Name two main differences between an optical zoom lens and a digital zoom.

6. Why would a videographer sometimes want to turn off the automatic focus feature of a camcorder?

7. Explain what white balance is and why we need to use it.

8. What function does the "Record Review" button provide?

9. Name two situations in which the use of camcorder outputs would be important.

10. List the six shots of the videography repertoire.

11. What is the main distinction between a bust shot and a close-up of a person?

12. Imagine you are making an instructional video program about the following three topics. For each topic, list an important detail that you would wish to include (a shot that would require a close-up).

   • How to inflate a bicycle tire.

   • How to sew a button onto a shirt.

   • How to brush your teeth.

13. How can you create depth in your video shots?

14. In tripod movements, how are a "truck" and a "dolly" similar? How are they different?

Student Project Plan

Growing Up

Description of Completed Project

The finished project will be a one- to two-minute video program made from 10 to 15 photographs of you growing up. The first picture should be from birth or infancy. The last picture should be you as you are now. A soundtrack will be added to the finished video.

Method

1. Gather 10 to 15 photographs from family albums or collections. Try to use photos that show important events in your life (birth, first birthday, first day of school, family gatherings or events). Number them with pencil on the back in the order that you will videotape them.

2. Create a title for your project. You may use a character generator or a title card, depending on your teacher's decision.

3. Now it's time to record your project. With the lens caps on, record about 15 seconds of video. This will be your "black" before the program begins.

4. With the camcorder on a tripod, record your title card for 8 to 10 seconds. Fade in on the title card.

5. Videotape each photo for at least eight seconds. If you are using a script, make sure to record the photo long enough to read the script slowly. Fade out on the last photograph.

6. Place the lens cap on the camcorder, and record at least 10 more seconds of black.

7. Preview the videotape to make sure there are no problems. If there are problems, simply re-create the project.

8. Add the soundtrack to the tape using the method selected by the teacher.

Evaluation

The completed project will be worth 100 points.

- Photo selection (20 points)
- Title (20 points)
- Camera work (20 points)
- Soundtrack (20 points)
- Overall production (20 points)

Evaluation Sheet: Growing Up

NAME _____ DATE _____

Photo Selection

    Depicts life span . . . . (10 points) _____

    Variety of events. . . . . (10 points) _____

Title

    Appropriate and clever . . . . (10 points) _____

    Color balance/contrast . . . . (10 points) _____

Camera Work

    Framed correctly. . . . . (10 points) _____

    Focus, steady . . . . (10 points) _____

Soundtrack

    Appropriate . . . . (10 points) _____

    Sound levels, fade. . . . . (10 points) _____

Overall Production

    Smooth, glitch free . . . . (10 points) _____

    Timely, meets objectives . . . . (10 points) _____

    Total Points Awarded . . . . (Out of 100) _____

Teacher Comments:

Student Project Plan

Camera Shots

Description of Completed Project

The completed project will be a video program that demonstrates your ability to create the shots in the videography repertoire. All shots should display proper videography technique as discussed in the chapter.

Method

1. Place the lens cap on your camcorder and record 10 to 15 seconds of black.

2. Record each shot on the Assignment Sheet/Evaluation Sheet. Make sure to indicate the order of shots in the "Sequence" column. There will be no editing on this project, so plan to do your best work. Set up each shot, then record.

3. Record each shot for 10 seconds.

4. After your last shot, place the lens cap back on the camcorder and record another 10 seconds of black.

5. Submit the videotape and the Assignment Sheet/Evaluation Sheet to your instructor for grading.

Evaluation

The completed project will be worth 100 points. Each shot is worth 10 points.

Assignment Sheet/Evaluation Sheet Camera Shots

NAME _____ DATE _____

Camera Shot	Sequence	Teacher Comments	Points (10)
Long shot			
Medium shot			
Bust shot			
Close-up			
Extreme close-up			
Over-the-shoulder shot			
Headroom Create a new shot from the list above that displays the appropriate amount of headroom.			
Leadroom Display the proper amount of lead room in a shot in which someone walks in from one side of the room to the other side.			
Rule of Thirds Create a shot that displays the Rule of Thirds.			
Depth Create a shot with foreground, middle ground, and background.			

2 MICROPHONES

Objectives

After successfully completing this chapter, you will be able to

- describe the main characteristics of any microphone: directionality, element, impedance, and frequency response.
- describe a variety of microphone formats and name several situations that would require the use of each microphone.
- demonstrate the proper use of microphones.
- create an on-camera interview segment using a camcorder, a microphone, and a tripod.

Vocabulary

condenser microphone. A microphone that contains an element made of two small vibrating magnetized plates.

dynamic microphone. A microphone that contains an element consisting of a diaphragm and moving coil.

lavaliere microphone. A small condenser microphone used in television production.

microphone. An audio component that converts sound waves into electrical energy.

omnidirectional. A microphone pickup pattern in which the microphone "hears" equally well from all sides.

pressure zone microphone (PZM). A microphone consisting of a metal or plastic plate and a small microphone element. A PZM collects and processes all sound waves that strike the metal plate.

shotgun microphone. A microphone with an extremely directional pickup pattern.

unidirectional. A microphone pickup pattern in which the microphone processes most of its signal from sound collected in front of the microphone and very little from the sides and back.

windscreen. a form-fitting foam cover for the top of the microphone that eliminates the rumbling sound caused by wind and sudden bursts of air.

wireless microphone system. A microphone system consisting of a microphone, an FM transmitter, and a tuned receiving station that eliminates the need for long runs of microphone cable.

In this chapter, we'll learn about the basic instrument for collecting sound: the microphone. As the camcorder does for video, the microphone provides most of the audio that you will use in your video projects and reports. Microphones can be used to record a reporter's facts, a guest's comments, the roar of the crowd, and the subtle tones of a string quartet.

Because microphones need to collect so many types of sound from so many different sources, it's important to understand that not all microphones are designed to work in the same setting. There is no "best" or "perfect" microphone for all situations. A microphone that would be great for the pep rally would be a poor choice for a concert. Correct use of the microphone requires selection as well as technique.

For this reason, the words "collection" and "selection" are important in using microphones. It is important for schools to have a collection of different microphones for different situations. The student must select the best microphone for the situation. Just as a fisherman has a variety of lures in his tackle box, a good audio technician should have various microphones to choose from and the knowledge of how to choose the best for any situation.

Microphone Characteristics

In the pages that follow, we'll learn about the characteristics and functions of various microphones. We'll also cover some simple tips for using them.

Microphone Directionality

Think about the camcorder. What is the directionality of the camcorder? Of course, your answer is "straight ahead." You point the camcorder and record whatever is straight ahead! You don't record what is behind you or around the corner.

Oddly enough, not all microphones are straight ahead. Sure, some microphones collect sound from the front, but others collect sound from all around you. The two main microphone directionalities are omnidirectional and unidirectional (Figure 2.1).

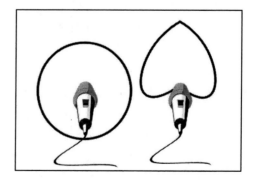

Fig. 2.1. Omnidirectional and unidirectional pickup patterns.

Omnidirectional Microphones

Omnidirectional microphones collect sound from all around them—a 360-degree area. Imagine you are a member of a singing group and the group is standing in a circle. You could hold the omnidirectional microphone in the center of the group, and all voices would be collected at the same volume. Omnidirectional microphones are also useful when collecting ambient sound (sound from the environment) and interviewing a group of people who might decide to talk all at the same time. Elementary school teachers often give omnidirectional microphones to their students for on-camera interviews because the children do not have to worry about "pointing" the microphone.

Unidirectional Microphones

The other type of microphone directionality is unidirectional. The "omni" in omnidirectional means "all." As you can probably guess, the "uni" in unidirectional means "one." The unidirectional microphone picks up sound from the top of the microphone, very little from the sides, and almost none from the back. The unidirectional microphone must be pointed at the source of the sound. You might want to think of the pickup pattern of the unidirectional microphone as being heart-shaped. For this reason, these microphones are also called a "cardioid" microphone. (*Cardi* is a Latin root word for "heart.") It takes a certain amount of skill and practice to use a unidirectional microphone. Imagine you are videotaping an on-camera interview using a unidirectional microphone. As you become engaged in the topic with your guest, you forget to point the microphone at the person speaking—that is, at yourself, and then at your guest. What sound will be recorded on the videotape? Your voice will be loud and clear, but the guest's response will be much lower in volume. Using a unidirectional microphone isn't a hard skill to learn, and with practice, pointing the microphone at the person speaking becomes second nature.

Unidirectional microphones have certain degrees of strength. The "classic" heart-shaped unidirectional microphone is most often found on handheld microphones. Later in this chapter, we'll look at a shotgun microphone, which is a unidirectional microphone with a very strong, narrow, and far-reaching pickup pattern.

Most microphones come with a brief printed manual that contains a simple drawing of the pickup pattern. If you can't find that drawing, you can probably visit the manufacturer's Web site and download the specifications for your microphones. Whether you need an omnidirectional or a unidirectional microphone, make sure you know its directionality before you begin your video project.

Microphone Element

In Chapter 1, we mentioned that a microphone changes sound waves into electrical signals. This task is accomplished by the microphone element. You will probably encounter two types of microphone elements in your television production class, the dynamic element and the condenser element.

Dynamic Element

The dynamic element is commonly found in inexpensive handheld microphones. Sound waves (changes in air pressure) enter the dynamic microphone, and a small coil of wire detects those waves and vibrates, generating a small amount of electricity. Dynamic microphones are generally durable—although you don't want to drop them, they will withstand an occasional drop or bump without damage. Dynamic microphones are also very good at recording loud noises. A dynamic microphone would be great for a report at a pep rally or an airport. You can capture very loud sounds without them becoming distorted.

Dynamic microphones provide average to good sound quality. They are fine for recording voice and ambient sound (such as the sound at a baseball game or playground) but wouldn't provide the sound you would want to record a singer or musical instrument. Because dynamic microphones are best suited for reporters, they are usually handheld microphones.

Condenser Element

The other type of microphone that you will find in school television studios uses a condenser element. In a condenser microphone, the sound waves cause two small, thin plates (often thin strips of metal) to vibrate close to each other. This vibration takes place in an electronic field. The small changes in the electronic field are translated into the electrical signal that is recorded onto the videotape.

Condenser microphones produce much better sound quality than dynamic microphones. They are favorites of singers and instrumentalists. Condenser microphones are used on movie sets, television stages, and in newsrooms to capture the excellent quality sound that we desire on our programs.

Fig. 2.2. This condenser microphone uses a 9-volt battery.

Condenser microphones are also more fragile than dynamic microphones. A drop might damage one of the thin plates inside the element. Condenser microphones also don't perform very well in loud environments. A loud sound will quickly result in distortion, but they are great for picking up very light, soft sounds that the dynamic element might miss altogether. For these reasons, condenser microphones are often used in controlled situations.

Condenser microphones require a power source (Figure 2.2). Frequently that power source is a battery (small batteries such as watch batteries and AAA batteries are often used). Sometimes condenser microphones require phantom power, which is power provided by an audio mixer. If you have a microphone that requires phantom power, you probably won't be able to use it with your camcorder (no phantom power there!). Schools usually select microphones that use batteries so that they don't have to worry about phantom power.

Condenser elements can be found in a variety of microphone styles: handheld, shotgun, lavaliere (tie-pin), and more. We'll look at specific microphone formats later in this chapter.

Before leaving our discussion of microphone elements, it's important for you to realize that microphones have several characteristics, including directionality and element. If you go to the microphone storage area in your studio, you might find an omnidirectional, dynamic microphone - good for interviewing a group. You might also find a unidirectional condenser microphone that would be a great choice for recording a violin solo. All of your microphones can be described by each of the category that we discuss. The first two were directionality and element. Now we'll look at the final two – impedance and frequency response.

Microphone Impedance

Generally speaking, audio (sound) systems—microphones and audio mixers—use one of the two types of signals: high impedance and low impedance. The impedance relates to the amount of resistance in the signal. High- and low-impedance signals are not compatible. Remember, microphones can be described as either high impedance or low impedance.

High-impedance microphones are often used in portable systems. Your camcorder's microphone jack is probably high impedance, requiring a high-impedance microphone. If you have a small, inexpensive audio mixer, you probably need to use high-impedance microphones.

Low-impedance microphones are usually used in professional systems. Professional-quality camcorders usually have low-impedance microphone jacks, and therefore, a low-impedance microphone must be used. You'll also find that professional audio mixers and public address systems (such as a school intercom system) will use low-impedance microphones. A few microphones have "switchable impedance." In other words, the microphone has a switch that lets you select high or low impedance.

The low-impedance signal usually results in a higher-quality (better-sounding) audio signal, but a lot of that depends on the quality of the microphone—and the speakers! Low-impedance signals can also travel farther (using longer cords) than high impedance. High-impedance signals begin to decrease and fade after a distance of about 30 feet. So if you need to string microphone cable more than 30 feet, you would be advised to use a low-impedance system.

Here's one of those "almost always" statements—low-impedance microphones use three-pronged XLR connectors. High-impedance microphone use ¼ inch phone plugs, or 1/8 inch mini plugs (Figure 2.3). That's an "almost always." Sometimes you'll encounter exceptions to the rule. If in doubt, read the manual. As with directionality and element, you can't make this determination simply by looking at the microphone.

The important part of this section is this: impedance levels —high or low—are not compatible with each other. If you have a low-impedance microphone, it will not work well with a high-impedance system. The opposite is also true—a high-impedance microphone will not work well with a low-impedance system. Electronics dealers (such as RadioShack) sell impedance transformers—barrel-shaped adapters that convert impedance from high to low or low to high. These adapters sell for about $20.

Often, medium-to-large television production facilities (such as a high school, college, or local cable TV studios) will find that they need two collections of microphones—high and low impedance. Their inexpensive camcorders and portable audio mixers require high-impedance microphones, and their studio setups require low impedance microphones. Some small studios avoid this duplication by purchasing higher-level portable equipment that can use low impedance microphones. Selecting switchable impedance microphones can also be a partial solution.

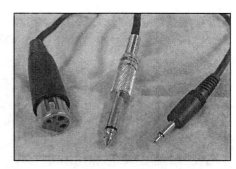

Fig. 2.3. Common microphone connectors: XLR, ¼" phone, 1/8" mini.

Microphone Frequency Response

The final microphone characteristic that deserves mention is frequency response. You know that sound travels through the air on sound waves, and all waves have a frequency. The lower the note (like a low note played on a tuba), the lower the frequency. A high note (the highest note played on a flute) has a much higher frequency.

You have probably had your hearing examined at school or in a doctor's office. You wear headphones, and an audiologist plays a variety of "beeps." Your job is to raise your hand as soon as you hear a beep. Some beeps are high (high frequency) and others are low (low frequency).

Just like your ears, microphones have frequencies that they can hear and frequencies that they can't hear. Some notes are just too low or too high for the microphone to hear. A great example is the telephone system in your house. The telephone doesn't play bass or treble notes very well. It only plays the middle frequencies. (That's why your telephone voice sounds fake, or "phony." The bass and treble characteristics of your voice are eliminated.)

Of course, you are looking for a microphone that has a greater frequency range—a microphone that can hear low notes and high notes, as well as the midrange. A microphone with a larger frequency range will sound better and capture the full range of sounds.

The typical human ear can hear sounds from 20 hertz to 20 kilohertz (20,000 hertz). That's a pretty wide range—from the lowest note on a pipe organ and the rumble of a train, to the highest tweet of a baby bird. Some microphones come pretty close to recording that wide range of sounds. Others do not. A quick glance at the microphone manual will tell you the frequency range.

As you probably guessed, condenser microphones usually have a larger frequency range than dynamic microphones. Dynamic microphones are fine for voice, but to capture the full range of musical notes in an orchestra, a condenser microphone would be required.

So now you can describe a microphone in four ways—the directionality, the element, the impedance, and the frequency range. Let's look at a couple of situations and decide which type of microphone would be best.

Situation 1: You are using your consumer-level camcorder to record an interview with the coach at a pep rally.

- **Directionality:** unidirectional. An omnidirectional would pick up too much background noise from the pep rally.

- **Element:** dynamic. A dynamic microphone could handle the loud noises of the pep rally. The high-quality sound of the condenser microphone just isn't necessary.

- **Impedance:** probably high impedance. Almost all consumer-level camcorders require high-impedance microphones. If in doubt, read the manual!

- **Frequency response:** probably not a factor in this situation. Of course, you want the best sound possible. The dynamic element limits this, but there are some great sounding dynamic microphones available.

Situation 2: A string quartet—two violins, a cello, and a string bass—are coming to your professional TV studio, and you really want to use only one microphone.

- **Directionality:** omnidirectional. One microphone placed in the center of the quartet would capture all of the players.

- **Element:** condenser. Condensers provide the best-quality sound and can pick up soft, subtle notes. Because the recording will be in a controlled environment, there's little danger of damaging the microphone.

- **Impedance:** probably low impedance, but check your audio system. The low-impedance system would let you videotape from farther away if needed and provide better sound quality.

- **Frequency response:** go for the best. Survey your school's collection of omnidirectional, condenser, low-impedance microphones and select the one with the best frequency response.

You can probably think of several other situations in your school. Remember, microphone use is about "collection" and "selection."

Types of Microphones (Microphone Formats)

Just as microphones are available with various directionalities, elements, impedance levels, and frequency responses, microphones are also available in various formats. The characteristics in the first part of this chapter describe how the microphones perform, but they don't tell us what they look like. Microphones come in various sizes and shapes, and you can probably find one to meet your needs in almost every situation.

As you read about the following microphone formats, remember that each microphone, no matter its size and shape, has the characteristics of directionality, element, impedance, and frequency response. You might even want to think of format as the fifth and final step in selecting a microphone.

Handheld Microphone

When most of us think of a microphone, we think of a handheld microphone—a microphone that the talent (the reporter or performer) holds in his or her hand (Figure 2.4). Handheld microphones are also found on microphone stands for use in panel discussions and music performances.

Handheld microphones are available in just about every combination of characteristics that you can imagine. A reporter would probable want a dynamic, unidirectional handheld microphone. A singer might want a condenser, unidirectional handheld microphone. A choir could use a condenser, omnidirectional handheld microphone on a stand.

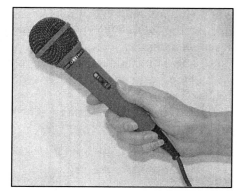

Fig. 2.4. Handheld microphone.

Handheld microphones are available in high, low, and switchable impedance. You can buy an excellent-sounding handheld microphone with a very wide frequency response (very low to very high) or a handheld microphone with a very narrow frequency response, like the microphone that is used by a child's toy cassette recorder. You can buy a decent-quality microphone suitable for use by a high school reporter for less than $25. The handheld microphone used by your favorite musical performer probably costs hundreds of dollars. Most handheld microphones fall somewhere in between those extremes.

Lavaliere (Tie-Pin) Microphone

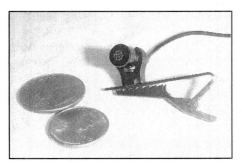

Fig. 2.5. Lavaliere microphone.

A lavaliere microphone is a very small microphone that is usually attached to the talent's clothing (Figure 2.5), usually with an alligator clip or a stick-pin with a clasp on the back. Lavaliere microphones are sometimes call tie-pin microphones because they resemble the tie-pins that well-dressed men wore in the past.

Lavaliere microphones are almost always omnidirectional, and they almost always have condenser elements. The battery required by the condenser element is usually found in a small box that's part of the microphone cable. A wide variety of batteries is used, from small watch batteries to 9-volt batteries.

There are three advantages to using a lavaliere microphone. First, they are small, and the viewer doesn't usually notice the microphone in the shot. News anchors prefer the lavaliere microphone over a handheld microphone on a mic stand. Second, they allow the talent to use his or her hands. In cooking shows, home handyman shows, and sports programs, this hands-free advantage is critical. The third advantage is that a lavaliere microphone requires almost no skill from the user. It can be quickly clipped on a talk show guest or interview subject. For these reasons, lavaliere microphones are popular in the school setting.

When deciding to use a lavaliere microphone, realize that it is for a single user. Don't plan to use a lavaliere microphone as the only microphone for an interview or have your guests share a single lavaliere. The rule is, one lavaliere per person.

Interesting fact: lavaliere microphones weren't "invented," they "evolved" from handheld microphones. If you watch certain television programs from the 1950s or 1960s—cooking shows and weather broadcasts are good examples—you're likely to see handheld microphones dangling from the talent's neck using a cord or chain. Over the years, small microphones became available, and the lavaliere microphone was born.

Surface Mount Microphone

Sometimes we need to use a single microphone to record a group sitting around a conference table or working on a group project at school. For this reason, the surface mount microphone was invented. A surface mount microphone has no handle. It has a flat back designed to lay evenly on a table or other smooth surface (Figure 2.6). In fact, some surface mount microphones have rubber on the back to keep them from sliding. As you have probably deduced, surface mount microphones are omnidirectional. They can be either dynamic or condenser, high or low impedance, depending on the specific microphone design.

Fig. 2.6. Surface mount microphone.

Pressure Zone Microphone

Fig. 2.7. Pressure zone microphone (PZM).

The pressure zone microphone, or PZM, is another way to record sound from large groups (Figure 2.7). The PZM consists of a microphone pointed downward, close to a plastic or metal plate. The plate serves as a conductor for all sound that strikes it, and the sound is sent directly to the microphone. A PZM can be placed flat on a table to pick up sound from everyone sitting around the table. Because they are flat, PZM microphones can serve as hidden microphones in dramatic videos. Some elementary schools use a PZM to record two newsreaders during a school news show using their camcorder's single microphone jack. PZMs can also be used effectively to record school bands, orchestras, or vocal music groups. The music director can mount one or two PZMs flat against the front wall of the practice room—like hanging a picture. In effect, the wall becomes a giant PZM microphone. As the group performs, the PZM microphone will receive all of the sound that strikes the front wall evenly.

Here's something you've probably already thought of: when a group is using a PZM or a surface mount microphone while sitting around a table, no one can tap the tabletop or kick the table legs. Such unwanted sounds will be expertly received by the microphone! Even though group participants don't need to worry about operating the microphone, the audio technician should warn them about the subconscious "tap-tap-tap" of a pencil on the tabletop, for example, which would ruin an otherwise excellent recording.

Shotgun Microphone

Earlier in this chapter, we described the unidirectional (cardioid) microphone, a microphone designed to collect most of its sound from the front, very little from the sides, and no sound from the back. What if you had a "super-cardioid" microphone—one that collected sound only from a very narrow area in front of the microphone and none at all from the sides or back? This would be a shotgun microphone. The word "shotgun" is a good way to describe this microphone. The shotgun microphone resembles the barrel of a shotgun in shape (Figure 2.8). Also like a shotgun, you must carefully aim this microphone to pick up the specific sound that you want. A good shotgun microphone can pick up a single voice in a crowded room. For this reason, the audio technician should always wear headphones when using this type of microphone.

Fig. 2.8. Shotgun microphone.

Shotgun microphones are great for videotaping guest speakers or presentations when the videographer is at the back of the classroom. You can probably think of other applications for a shotgun microphone as well. Reporters often use shotgun microphones in noisy environments, such as pep rallies, convention floors, and airport runways. A regular unidirectional microphone would pick up too much background noise in these settings. A shotgun microphone mounted on top of the camcorder is popular for the "in your face" style of reporting. The microphone is mounted right above the zoom lens and records whatever the videographer is videotaping. A shotgun microphone mounted on a long poll (a boom) can be raised above the talent for recording dramatic videos.

Shotgun microphones are almost always condenser type and can be either low impedance or high impedance. Some shotgun microphones have a three-way switch—off, cardioid, and super-cardioid. This way, they can be used in a variety of situations.

Wireless Microphone Systems

Fig. 2.9. A wireless microphone system includes a microphone, a transmitter, and a receiving station.

A wireless microphone system eliminates the length of cable between the microphone and the camcorder or audio mixer. That cable is replaced by a radio signal. The wireless microphone system consists of three devices—the microphone, the transmitter, and the receiving station (Figure 2.9).

The microphone is plugged into the transmitter, which is a small box, usually with a belt clip. The transmitter sends a signal to the receiving station. The receiving station is connected to the camcorder or to the audio mixer (in studio settings).

Wireless microphone systems are great when a long cable run is either impractical or impossible. A reporter walking through a crowd could use a wireless microphone system. So could a singer performing the National Anthem at a sports event. You can probably think of many applications for wireless microphone systems.

Wireless microphones can be either handheld or lavaliere. Some handheld wireless microphone systems have the transmitter installed in the handle of the microphone. Some systems include both a handheld and a lavaliere microphone, allowing for uses in multiple situations. When using a wireless microphone system, realize that you still must select the best microphone for the situation. The "wireless" aspect is simply another choice for the audio technician.

Early wireless microphone systems were not very dependable and often had static and "hum" problems. Modern systems, however, can give good service and are replacing regular "wired" microphones in many settings, such as churches, auditoriums, and gymnasiums.

The audio technician has an extra responsibility when using a wireless microphone system—power. The transmitter needs a power supply, and so does the receiving station. Because it is designed to be portable, the transmitter almost always uses a battery. Some receiving stations use a battery, and others require power from a wall outlet. (Some can use either.) This is an important consideration for using a wireless system. If your wireless microphone system requires a power outlet, you will probably not be able to use it for remote locations. Here's another power issue: wireless microphone transmitters and receivers drain batteries quickly. Plan to carry extra batteries on remote shoots. Wireless microphone owners usually invest in a rechargeable battery system.

If you plan to use a wireless microphone system, practice with it, just as you practiced with your camcorder before going on your first big shoot. Know your wireless microphone's range—how far the signal can travel without being distorted. Some systems claim a range of a quarter mile or more. That range can quickly be reduced by walls, fluorescent lights, power lines, trees, bad weather, and a variety of other factors, however, so keep this in mind.

Using Microphones

Selecting the right microphone is important. It is also important to use microphones correctly. Here are some tips that should help.

Know your Microphones

Your school might own several microphones—from the studio lavalieres used during a news show to the shotgun microphone used by the remote camera crew at football games. Learn about each microphone to which you have access and gain experience with it.

Use Headphones

Would you operate your camcorder without a view-finder or viewscreen? Of course not! How would you know what you are videotaping? Yet you might be surprised to know how many audio technicians forget the headphones when videotaping a simple interview. (During simple recording sessions, the videographer probably also has audio responsibilities.) Make sure to include headphones in every videotaping scenario that requires sound (Figure 2.10).

Fig. 2.10. Headphones are important when an external microphone is used.

Handle Your Microphones Carefully

Although they appear sturdy, and most of us have seen popular performers abuse their microphones, remember that microphones can be easily damaged. Think of your microphone like an egg or a light bulb. Drop it, and it will probably be damaged. A microphone should never be used as a prop. Never throw or mistreat a microphone for "effect." Unlike top-selling singers, we don't have the money to replace our microphones after every use!

Part of microphone care involves the cable. Many microphone problems are the result of abused cables. A microphone cable seems somewhat thick, but most of that thickness is insulation. The copper wire inside is actually quite thin. Stepping on the cable, closing a door on the cable, or twisting the cable tightly for storage can damage that thin copper wire. Some microphones have the cable permanently attached. If this cable becomes damaged, then the microphone is probably destined for the trashcan.

Testing by Speaking

How do you test a microphone? Simply speak into it. Never, NEVER tap the surface of a microphone, which will damage it. Tapping the microphone to test it is a myth made popular by TV and movies. In the real world, we don't do that!

Carefully Connect Your Microphone

Your camcorder's microphone jack can be damaged by careless microphone connection. Make sure to insert your microphone gently into the camcorder's microphone jack. A broken microphone jack can send the camcorder to the repair shop for an expensive repair that can be easily avoided.

Here's a frequent problem: the microphone plug and microphone jack are different sizes. Typically, the microphone has a quarter-inch phone plug, and the microphone jack is 1/8-inch mini. (The variety of microphone plugs and jacks is discussed extensively in the next chapter.) The solution seems easy—use an adapter to convert the microphone plug to 1/8-inch mini. The problem lies in the combined weight of the microphone cable, plug, and adapter. All of this weight rests on the tiny microphone jack. Over time, this will destroy the jack and require repair. Instead of using an adapter, select a six-foot cable that receives the phone plug of the microphone and has an 1/8-inch mini plug on the other end. This way, the only weight on the camcorder's microphone jack is that of the mini plug. The microphone cable and the heavy phone plug rest on the floor.

Use a Windscreen when Recording Outdoors

A windscreen is a piece of foam rubber that fits over your microphone (Figure 2.11). The windscreen cuts down on severe bursts of air caused by the wind. A windscreen should be used any time you are videotaping outdoors. Without it, the wind will cause a rumbling sound in your microphone.

If your talent has an especially expressive voice, emphasizing the "explosive" sounds of "b," "d," "p," and "t," consider using a windscreen indoors as well.

Sometimes a windscreen is included with the microphone. More frequently, the windscreen is a separate purchase. Windscreens usually cost less than $2 and are worth the expense.

Fig. 2.11. Using a microphone outdoors? Use a windscreen!

Use the Correct Talent-to-Microphone Distance

When using a handheld or lavaliere microphone, the microphone should be four to six inches from the source. Any closer, and the sound becomes distorted. Any farther, and the sound is hollow, lacking the bass and treble tones that we like to hear.

Mic a Source, Not an Area

When possible, place your microphone near the source of the sound, not just in the general area. This will provide your recordings with the rich sound that you desire and will eliminate much of the background noise.

Summary

Audio is an important part of video production, and the microphone is an important tool for collecting good sound. The keys to proper microphone use are knowing the microphones in your collection, selecting the best microphone for your recording situation, and using that microphone properly. With the wide variety of microphones available, you can record great audio for your video projects.

Selected Manufacturer Web Sites

Audio-technica http://www.audio-technica.com
Crown http://www.crownaudio.com
RadioShack http://www.radioshack.com
Shure http://www.shure.com

Review Questions

1. Name the four characteristics used to describe the performance of a microphone.

2. Briefly explain the difference between an omnidirectional and a unidirectional pattern.

3. Which characteristic of a dynamic microphone makes it a frequent choice of news reporters?

4. What benefit does a condenser microphone provide that a dynamic microphone does not?

5. Phantom power is provided by _____.

6. What type of connector is almost always used by low-impedance microphones?

7. What is the frequency range that the human ear can hear?

8. For each situation that follows, name the directionality (omnidirectional or unidirectional) and element (dynamic or condenser) that describes the microphone you would select for audio recording.

    • A vocal trio standing onstage sharing a microphone

    • An interview near an airport runway

    • Providing a microphone for a flute solo

    • An interview with the starting lineup of the basketball team

9. What are the three advantages to using a lavaliere microphone?

10. What is the main difference between the surface-mount microphone and the PZM microphone?

11. List three situations in which you would use a shotgun microphone in your video production.

12. Name the three elements of the wireless microphone system.

13. How should you test a microphone?

14. In your own words, describe why it is important to have access to a collection of different microphones.

Student Project Plan

Interview

Description of Completed Project

The finished project will be a one- to two-minute interview with anyone who comes to school on a daily basis. The video will consist of a two-person medium shot, and the audio will be the actual interview.

Method

1. Each student should select the job he or she would like to perform—interviewer or videographer. Students then select a partner and form a team.

2. The team selects a person to interview (the guest) and schedules the interview.

3. The team formulates a list of three open-ended questions and shares the questions with the guest at least one day prior to the interview.

4. The interview is videotaped. Make sure to roll at least five seconds of videotape before the interview, and five more seconds of videotape after the interview.

5. The team views and critiques the interview.

6. Interviews are shown to the class and evaluated by the teacher.

Evaluation

The completed project will be worth 150 points for each student.

- The interviewer will earn 75 points based on microphone technique, questioning skills, camera presence (eye contact, posture, etc.), and format/script.

- The videographer will earn 75 points based on videography (the proper shot), camera steadiness, five seconds before and after, and background/location.

- A 75-point general impression grade will be awarded to each team member.

Example 43

Interview Format Sheet

Hello. Our guest today on _____ (name of program) is

_____(guest name). _____ (Guest name) is

_____(reason you are interviewing them).

Three open-ended questions—questions that cannot be answered with a "yes" or "no."

Thank you _____ (guest name), and _____

_____ (friendly ending). For _____ (name of program),

I'm _____ (interviewer's name).

Example

Hello, our guest today on "Meet the Teacher" is Ms. Pat Franklin. Ms. Franklin is our media specialist at Central High School, and the media center has just received some new award-winning books.

Ms. Franklin, exactly what awards have these new books won?

Who decides which books win these awards?

How can students find these new books when they come to the media center?

Thanks, Ms. Franklin. I'm sure our students are looking forward to reading these great new books from our media center. For *Falcon Focus,* I'm Joey Armstrong.

Evaluation Sheet: Interview

NAME _____ DATE _____

Interviewer

Microphone technique . . . . (20 points) _____
Quality of questions . . . . (20 points) _____
Camera presence (eye contact, posture, etc.) . . . . . . (20 points) _____
Format and script . . . . (15 points) _____
Subtotal for Interviewer . . . . **(Out of 75)** _____

Videographer

Shot composition . . . . (20 points) _____
Steady shot . . . . (20 points) _____
Background/location . . . . (20 points) _____
Five seconds (before and after) . . . . (15 points) _____
Subtotal for Videographer . . . . **(Out of 75)** _____

Group

General impression . . . . (Out of 75) _____

Final Grades

Interviewer _____ + _____ = _____
Videographer _____ + _____ = _____

Teacher Comments:

3 ADVANCED AUDIO EQUIPMENT AND TECHNIQUES

Objectives

After successfully completing this chapter, you will be able to

- identify and describe the main operational controls of an audio mixer.
- identify several audio sources for video production and describe the appropriate use of each source.
- identify various audio connectors and how they are used in video production.
- explain the processes of audio mixing and audio dubbing.
- explain the concept of production music in a video production setting and list several reasons for using production music.
- compose a script for video production.
- produce an audio commercial.

Vocabulary

adapter. A device used to achieve compatibility between two items of audio/video equipment.

audio dub. An editing technique that involves erasing the existing audio track on a videotape and replacing it with a new one.

audio mixer. An electronic component that facilitates the selection and combination of audio signals.

balance (also "pan"). A potentiometer that lets the technician send each input to either the right or left channel on a stereo audio mixer.

cue. An audio mixer function that allows the user to hear an audio source (usually through headphones) without selecting that source for broadcast or recording; the audio counterpart of a preview monitor.

fader (also "fader bar"). An audio mixer level control that slides vertically (up and down), with "up" increasing the level and "down" decreasing the level.

potentiometer (also "pot"). An audio mixer level control; a dial that moves clockwise and counterclockwise. Moving the pot clockwise (toward the right) increases the level, and moving the pot counterclockwise (toward the left) decreases the level.

production music. Musical selections created specifically for use in audio and video programs. When customers buy production music, they also buy copyright permissions not granted with standard music purchases, thus averting copyright violations.

trim (also "gain"). An audio mixer control (usually a potentiometer) that lets the audio technician adjust each individual microphone so that all microphones will perform at the same level.

volume unit (VU) meter. A device used to measure the intensity of an audio signal.

In Chapter 2, you learned about microphones and their importance in television production. Topics including microphone characteristics, microphone format, microphone selection, and proper microphone use were covered. Sometimes, though, recording audio for a television program requires more than a simple microphone-to-camcorder connection.

Let's look at an example: you've been hired as the audio technician for a popular talk show. You're familiar with the format—two or three guests are seated on the stage. Sometimes the host sits with the guests, and other times he or she walks through the studio to give the audience members a chance to ask questions and offer comments. Theme music is an important part of this show, and small sections of the theme song are played as the show breaks for commercials. Typically, a videotaped segment is played during the program, and you need to be able to record the audio from that videotape onto the final program.

If you read Chapter 2, you've probably already decided which microphones to use. The guests would be best served by lavaliere microphones. The lavalieres are so small that they wouldn't be obvious in close-ups, and using a lavaliere would free guests from using proper microphone technique. You could use wireless lavaliere microphones, if available. The program host would need a handheld wireless unidirectional microphone to make traveling through the studio audience safe and possible.

But where would these microphones plug in? A show like this would probably use two or three video cameras. Would you plug a microphone into each camera? What about the theme song and the sound from the VCR?

The answer: You would use an audio mixer.

An audio mixer is an electronic component that allows a technician (that's you) to select and combine audio sources. All of the audio sources mentioned—the host's microphone, the guests' microphones, the VCR, and the CD player (for the theme song) would be connected to inputs on the audio mixer. The output of the audio mixer is connected to a VCR, and this VCR will record the video and audio signal at the same time. (Video mixing is described in Chapter 4.)

In this chapter, we look at the basic and advanced features that you'll find on audio mixers. We also discuss some of the audio sources that you can connect to an audio mixer. This chapter also includes sections on mixing voice and music, production music, and scriptwriting tips. That's a lot of territory to cover, so let's get started!

Audio Mixer

Fig. 3.1. An audio mixer.

As we stated earlier, an audio mixer is an electronic component that allows the audio technician to select and combine audio sources (Figure 3.1). All of the audio sources (microphones, VCRs, music sources) are connected to inputs in the audio mixer. The technician can select which source the audience hears by raising the level of one source (for example, a microphone) and turning off the other sources. The audio technician can also combine sources, raising the levels of two, three, or even all the sources at once.

Let's look again at our talk show example. The show begins with a theme song, so the audio technician raises the level of the CD player and plays the CD containing the song. As it ends, the host begins to speak. The audio technician raises the level of the host's microphone and slowly fades out the theme song. The host introduces each guest, and they all say a quick "hello" to the audience. The audio technician raises the levels of the guests' microphones, so that the "hellos" are heard and recorded. The audio technician quickly lowers the guests' microphone levels so that their nervous coughs are not heard. The host introduces the talk show topic with a prerecorded videotape. The audio technician raises the level of the VCR as the videotape segment plays and lowers the level of the host's microphone, so that the host can talk to the director off camera.

At this point, you're probably realizing two things: first, the audio technician is a very busy person, and you're right! The previous paragraph describes only the first three minutes of our talk show, and already the audio technician has made several important moves. A mistake on any of these tasks would be obvious to the audience and embarrassing for the host. That brings us to the second realization—the audio technician needs to know what's going to happen on the program before it happens. The audio technician can't react. She or he has to know the order of events of the program: the theme song, the host's introduction, the guests' greetings, the videotaped segment. Therefore, the audio technician needs to be involved in every part of program planning, from start to finish.

Basic Audio Mixer Features

Now, let's take a closer look at the audio mixer and learn about the features available on most, if not all, audio mixers.

Inputs

One of the most important characteristics of an audio mixer is its inputs—in other words, what can you plug into it? What kinds of signals can the audio mixer handle? The two most common types of inputs are microphone inputs and line inputs (Figure 3.2).

As the name indicates, microphones are connected to the microphone inputs. Some audio mixers have only high-impedance microphone inputs, some have only low-impedance microphone inputs, and some have both. Of course, the impedance of the microphone must match the impedance of the microphone input. Usually (although not

Fig. 3.2. Inputs on this audio mixer include XLR and quarter-inch phone.

always) low-impedance inputs use the three-pronged XLR plug, and high-impedance microphones use the quarter-inch phone jack. Another important consideration is the number of microphone inputs that your audio mixer can offer. Some smaller audio mixers may have only two or three microphone inputs. Of course, the audio technician would be extremely limited in the types of programs that he or she could produce with this audio mixer.

The other type of input is the line input. CD players, audiocassette players, VCRs, and MP3 players can all be connected to the audio mixer's line inputs. Again, the number of inputs is critical. A smaller audio mixer could have only one or two line inputs. This could be a problem when attempting to mix the audio for a complex television show. Line inputs are usually indicated on an audio mixer by a pair of RCA phono plugs, also known as patch cords. The two cords are used to transfer a stereo signal—left and right channel.

Level Controls

The ability to make some sounds louder and others softer is a key feature of the audio mixer. This is accomplished using the level controls. Two types of level controls are commonly used in audio mixers— fader bars, and potentiometers ("pots"). Fader bars slide vertically (up and down), with "up" increasing and "down" decreasing the level (Figure 3.3). Fader bars are popular with audio technicians because they can slide two or more of the bars at once, each of which controls sound levels from a different source.

Fig. 3.3. Fader bar.

On an audio mixer, each input has its own level control (fader bar or pot). The audio technician uses the level controls to select and combine the appropriate audio sources.

Fig. 3.4. Potentiometer ("pot") control.

Potentiometers, or pots, are found on smaller audio mixers. A pot is a dial that moves clockwise and counterclockwise (Figure 3.4). Moving the pot clockwise (toward the right) increases the level, and moving the pot counterclockwise (toward the left) decreases the level. As you can imagine, it is difficult to adjust more than one pot at a time. However, pots take up a much smaller space on an audio mixer and are frequently found on smaller audio mixers designed for remote location use.

There is also a master level control (fader or pot) that controls the overall audio output. When the master level control is set at zero (all the way down on a fader bar; all the way to the left on a pot), no sound will come out of the audio mixer, no matter how high the individual input levels are set. This master level control allows the audio technician to increase or decrease all of the levels quickly.

Before we leave this section on level controls, let's make sure we know the difference between level and volume. The level is the strength of the signal being sent to the output device. An appropriate level means that the sound is clean and clear, with no distortion. A level set too high will sound "fuzzy" and distorted. A level set too low will sound hollow and muted.

Volume is different. Volume is the loudness of the sound controlled by an amplifier and played through a speaker system. That amplifier could be a large amplifier in a public address system, or a small amplifier in a TV. Beginning audio technicians sometimes confuse these two characteristics of sound. For example, they might play a song on a CD player connected to one of their audio mixer inputs. The audio mixer is connected to a VCR, and the VCR is connected to a TV. The audio mixer is set to the proper level, but the sound coming out of the TV is not loud enough. What do they do? They increase the level on the audio mixer—BIG MISTAKE. Increasing the level will result in a distorted sound being recorded on the videotape. The sound on the TV will be louder, but it will be distorted. You probably know the correct action for our audio technician—simply turn up the volume on the TV. You would be surprised at how many times this mistake is made.

Volume Unit (VU) Meters

Okay, so you're convinced that you need to find the best level for each of your audio inputs, but how do you know the correct level? Fortunately, almost all audio mixers have volume unit meters, commonly called VU meters. A VU meter is an electronic device that displays the strength of an audio signal. VU meters have a setting that indicates 100%. The audio technician must adjust each input so that it peaks at 100% and never goes over that level. An audio signal above 100% sounds distorted. An audio signal that never approaches 100% sounds muffled. The audio technician must continually adjust the fader bars and pots to make sure the final output does not exceed 100% VU.

Two types of VU meters are commonly found on audio mixers: the LED (light emitting diode) display and the analog display. The LED display is a series of flashing lights that illuminate as the audio signal gets stronger (Figure 3.5). The stronger the signal, the more lights appear. Typically, the lights are color coded. Green lights are safe, but as the VU approaches 100%, yellow lights are used. The lights above 100% VU are red. This is the audio mixer's way of saying "STOP!"

Fig. 3.5. An LED VU (volume unit) meter.

The analog dial is like a car speedometer. The needle moves to the right as the audio level increases (Figure 3.6). The 100% VU setting is about three-fourths of the way across the dial. Usually, a red line is painted behind the needle to indicate 100%. More experienced audio technicians favor Analog VU meters. They can still be found on professional audio mixers, but most low-to-moderate priced models now have LED displays.

Fig. 3.6. Analog VU (volume unit) meter.

Outputs

Of course, the reason we're connecting audio sources and adjusting them to the proper levels is so that we can output our combined (or "mixed") audio signal to another device for recording or amplification. That's where the audio outputs come into play (Figure 3.7). We discuss the actual connection later in this chapter, but for now it's important to point out that good audio technicians know how many audio outputs they have to work with. In a typical TV production scenario, the audio output is sent to a VCR for recording along with the video signal. However, the audio technician might also be asked to send the signal to a public address system so that the studio audience can hear and to another audio system used by the show's director or technical director. Advanced audio mixers have at least two or three audio outputs. Lower level audio mixers have only one. These outputs might be labeled "output," "record output," or "send."

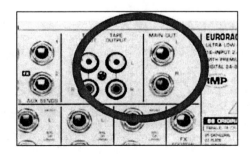

Fig. 3.7. Outputs on this audio mixer include an RCA phono plug and a ¼-inch phone.

Headphone Jack

Using the VU meters, it's easy to see whether the combined sound level is peaking at 100% VU. But how do you know whether the combination of sounds is right—that the music isn't too loud or the voice not loud enough? You have to listen, and nothing beats a set of headphones. Almost all audio mixers have a headphone jack so that you can use headphones to listen to the combination of audio inputs. Some headphone jacks are accompanied by a switch that lets the audio technician select the source of the sound played in the headphones. Using this switch, one can select the total mix or any one of the individual inputs. This lets the audio technician listen to each source, one at a time, and diagnose possible problems during shot production.

Stereo/Mono Switch

Most audio mixers provide stereo outputs, allowing the audio technician to send some sounds to the left channel/speaker and other sounds to the right channel/speaker. This stereo channel separation is rarely used in television production because a large percentage of the population (and most school audiences) are watching programs on a mono (single audio channel) television. The stereo/mono switch lets the audio technician select the stereo signal, creating different right and left channels, or the mono signal, in which the same sound is sent to both channels. The mono setting is a wise choice for most school applications.

Advanced Audio Mixer Features

Audio mixers vary greatly in price and function. A simple audio mixer with the features listed in the previous sections sells for $100 or less. Most audio technicians, however, prefer an audio mixer with most of the following advanced features.

Trim

Fig. 3.8. The trim pot, or gain control, is located right below each microphone input.

Earlier in this chapter, we mentioned the need to adjust microphone levels to peak at 100% VU. Most audio technicians know that different microphones have different output levels, however. Some microphones are "loud" and others provide a softer signal. Consequently, the fader bar for the first microphone might be all the way near the bottom (to compensate for its natural loudness), and the second microphone's fader bar will be near the top of the scale. Wouldn't it be great if we could adjust the input and make all microphone levels similar? That's what the trim function does. Trim (sometimes called "gain") is a control (usually a pot) that lets the audio technician adjust each microphone so that all of them will perform at the same level. "Loud" microphones can be "trimmed down," and soft microphones can be "trimmed up." The trim pot for each microphone is usually located right below or above that microphone's input jack (Figure 3.8).

Balance (Pan)

The balance control is a pot that lets the technician send each input to either the right or left channel on a stereo audio mixer. (Of course, a mono audio mixer will not have a balance feature.) When the pot is turned all the way to the left, the sound from that input will go only to the left stereo channel. When the pot is turned all the way to the right, the sound from that input will go only to the right channel. When the balance pot is in the "straight up" position, the sound from that input will go to both channels. This feature is also called "pan."

Because television production frequently uses mono signals, the balance pot is usually kept straight up for each input. However, you can probably imagine how a musical group would use the balance function to enhance their concert sound.

Equalization (EQ)

Equalization controls the amount of bass, midrange, and treble tones in the each audio input. Equalization is usually controlled by three pots—bass, midrange, and treble. The technician can adjust the EQ to make each input sound richer and fuller.

Some audio mixers offer equalization (EQ) for each individual input. Others equalize only the combined output signal, which has limited use.

Mute

This function, usually an on-off button near each input's fader bar, instantly mutes (turns off completely) that input. This is useful for microphones, which are typically not faded in or out.

Solo

The solo function is similar to mute, and the solo on-off button is usually right beside the mute button. As the name indicates, the solo button turns off all of the other inputs, making that single source the only audio input that is sent to the master. Basically, solo keeps itself on and instantly mutes all of the other inputs.

Cue

On some audio mixers, each audio input has a cue button. When the cue button (on-off) is depressed, that sound can be heard by selecting the "cue" position on the headphone jack switch. Imagine you are using a song on an audiocassette tape during your program, and you're not sure whether the audiocassette is cued to the right place. You can press the cue button on the audiocassette input (near the fader bar), switch the headphone selection to cue, and hear the audiocassette through the headphones. Because the fader bar for the audiocassette player is still all the way down, the audience won't hear the tape being cued. That sound is only played through the headphones.

Cross-Fader

Imagine a fader bar positioned between the bars for Input 1 and Input 2. Pushing the bar to the left would select only Input 1. Pushing the bar to the right would select only Input 2. When the bar is in the center position, both Input 1 and Input 2 can be heard. The audio technician can move the fader bar from one side to the other, fading in one input while fading out the other. This special fader bar is called a cross-fader. As you've probably guessed, a cross-fader would be valuable for a DJ who likes to fade between songs. The cross-fader has limited use in television production settings.

Send

The send control, usually a pot for each audio input, lets the audio technician send the signal to a special audio output called the send output. Using the send function, the audio technician can create a separate audio output (for example, recording on an audiocassette) on the audio mixer, totally independent of the audio mixer's main output. For example, an audio technician working with a musical group could create an audiocassette of just piano and vocals by turning up the send for only the vocalists' microphones and the microphone on the piano.

Digital Audio Effects

Another use for the send function allows the audio technician to send selected audio inputs to digital audio effects, such as reverb, echo, and delay. These digital audio effects are often preferred by singers. Some audio mixers have built-in digital audio effects. Other audio mixers accommodate separate digital audio effects units.

Audio Sources

In Chapter 2, we explored the different microphones that can be connected to your audio mixer. In this section, we'll look at other audio sources that are often connected as inputs to the audio mixer. The diagram (Figure 3.9) is provided to show you how each component is connected to the audio mixer.

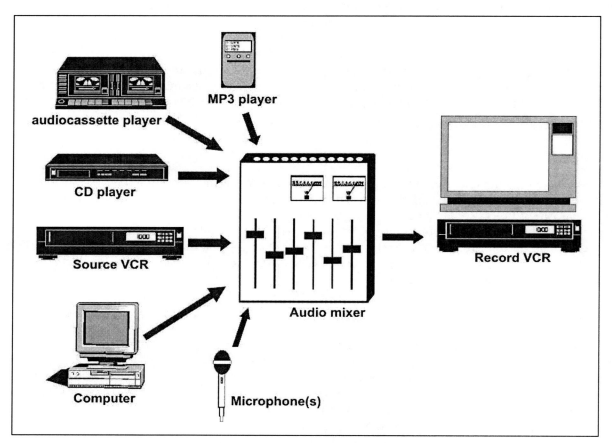

Fig. 3.9. Audio mixer connections.

VCR

News programs often include prerecorded videotaped segments. These might include interviews, sports highlights, or concert footage. All of these have sound that needs to be recorded on your final program. The VCR has audio output jacks, usually located on the back of the VCR. Use patch cords (a pair of RCA phono cords) to connect the VCR output to one of the line inputs on your audio mixer.

Compact Disc (CD) Players

Compact disc (CD) players are essential in most TV studios. The biggest advantage of the CD player is the instant track access. For the audio technician, track number 25 on the CD is only a few button pushes away. In years past, that spot would have to be found on an audiotape with no visual help from the display. Can you imagine a program producer handing you an audiocassette tape and telling you to play the 8th song, and then the 14th song? That would be almost impossible with an audiocassette, but no problem at all with a CD.

The CD player connects to the audio mixer with a set of patch cords. Locate the audio-out jacks on the back of the CD player and use a set of patch cords to connect that output to one of the line inputs on your audio mixer.

Audiocassette Players

So, if CDs are so great, why would we ever use an audiocassette? Many locally recorded audio segments are available only on audiocassette. An example would be your school's fight song or alma mater. You could record the band playing the fight song using an audiocassette recorder and play that audiocassette tape during the sports segment of your news show. You can probably think of several other uses for audiocassettes in your studio.

To connect an audiocassette player to your audio mixer, use a set of patch cords to connect the audio out of the audiocassette player to a line input on your audio mixer.

Of course, CD player-recorders are now becoming more affordable for schools. Most likely, the recordable CD will eventually replace the audiocassette in the school setting. Professional studios have already made this transition.

MP3 Players

Most students are probably familiar with portable MP3 players. MP3 is shorthand for the file designation MPEG-1 Audio Layer-3, as designed by the Motion Picture Experts Group (MPEG). MP3 is a digital file format used by computers. When a computer converts a file to MP3 (a process called "ripping") , it eliminates the data outside the normal range of human hearing and compresses the remaining data. This makes for a much smaller file size than other computer audio formats (such as .wav). These MP3 files can be stored on a hard drive or any other computer storage media, such as a memory stick or a compact flash card. Your portable MP3 player converts those files into audio that you can hear.

Of course, the MP3 format has a somewhat negative reputation in the music industry, as songs are ripped from CDs and traded over the Internet. However, the MP3 player has a legitimate use in the school television studio. Some music creation programs (discussed later in this chapter) let the user make original music with just a few mouse clicks. These songs can be saved in the MP3 format and downloaded onto an MP3 player for later use. Because MP3 is actually a computer file, expect the MP3 player to play an even greater role in future TV studios.

Computer

Your computer can also be an audio source for video production. Later in this chapter, we'll look at computer software that lets you create original music for your projects. Certainly you could burn this music on a compact disc, but you could also play it directly on the computer. Also, some Web sites offer royalty-free music and sound effects for student use. These resources can be played on your computer and integrated into your projects.

Audio Mixer Connectors

Audio equipment uses three types of connectors—the quarter-inch phone, RCA phono, and XLR. Let's take a quick look at each connector.

Quarter-inch Phone

The quarter-inch phone connector gets its name from its diameter and the fact that it was once used by telephone operators many years ago (Figure 3.10). Quarter-inch phone connectors are often used by high-impedance microphones—the microphone cable, and the microphone jack on the audio mixer. Musical instruments, such as guitars and keyboards, also use the quarter-inch phone plug to connect to amplifiers and audio mixers. These connectors can be either stereo or mono. The stereo (two-channel) connector has two black stripes on the plug shaft, and the mono (single channel) connector has only one stripe.

Fig. 3.10. A quarter-inch phone connector.

RCA Phono

The RCA phono connector is typically used to connect audio sources (for example, CD players and audiocassette players) to audio mixers and home stereo equipment. The RCA phono connector is capable of carrying only one signal. Therefore, a pair of these cables is necessary to achieve a stereo signal (Figure 3.11). A pair of RCA phono cords is called a patch cord. Patch cords use red and black connectors (or sometimes red and white connectors) to help the user connect the left and right channels properly. (The cables themselves are identical.) Expect to find RCA phono connectors on the outputs of audio sources and the line inputs on your audio mixer.

Fig. 3.11. An RCA phono connector.

XLR Connector

The XLR connector divides the audio signal into three sections (Figure 3.12). Each section is handled by a prong in the XLR connector. XLR connectors are typically found in low-impedance microphones and other low-impedance audio equipment.

Fig. 3.12. An XLR connector.

Other Connectors

In your audio work, you might encounter other types of audio connectors. The eighth-inch mini connector is similar in shape to the phone connector but only half the size. The mini connector is used in portable stereo equipment, such as MP3 players, and portable headphones. As the use of optical audio increases, you might also find optical connectors. The optical connector is used with special optical cable to connect digital audio components, such as CD recorders and minidisk players.

Adapters

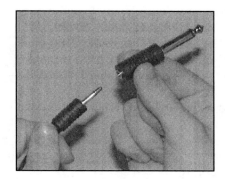

Fig. 3.13. Adapters can be used to change the connector type.

What happens if you need to change the type of connector to meet your audio mixer's input jacks? You can usually buy an adapter to make this conversion. For example, your microphone could have an eighth-inch mini connector, and your audio mixer has quarter-inch phone jacks. You would need an adapter that accepts the mini plug and converts it to phone plug (Figure 3.13). Most electronics stores have a wide assortment of adapters. All school TV studios should have a collection of commonly used adapters on hand when the need arises.

A final word about adapters—adapters don't change impedance. Imagine you have a high-impedance microphone with a quarter-inch phone connector and you want to use it with your low-impedance audio mixer, which has only XLR connectors. You could use an adapter that would convert the quarter-inch phone connector into the XLR connector, but you wouldn't be changing the impedance. Even though the microphone would now "fit" the audio mixer, the signal would still be the wrong impedance. Electronics stores sell a device called a matching line transformer that converts impedance. The matching line transformer looks just like the adapter—it converts the quarter-inch plug into an XLR plug—but the matching line transformer also changes the impedance. Remember—impedance isn't just about the shape of the connector; it is a fundamental property of the audio signal.

The Audio Mixer Outputs

Every audio mixer has at least one set of outputs. In school video production (and most other small-format production), these outputs are connected to the audio inputs on the recording VCR. Typically, this connection is made with patch cords. However, some high-end audio mixers and VCRs use phone or XLR connectors.

Some audio mixers may have several sets of outputs. As mentioned earlier, one set of outputs can be the "send" outputs. The audio technician can "send" any or all of the audio inputs to this set of outputs. Another set might be the "effects" output. These outputs would be connected to a digital audio effects unit to add reverb, echo, and so on. An audio mixer could have additional outputs, just for convenience. These outputs might be used infrequently, but the audio technician is glad that they're there if he needs them.

The Audio Dub Process

Some of your uses of an audio mixer will be in a "live" recording session, like a news show, a football game, or the talk show that we described earlier in this chapter. Sometimes, however, audio will be added at a later time, during what is called postproduction. The process of erasing the old audio track and replacing it with a new one is called audio dub.

Did you catch the two most important words in that last sentence? "Erasing" and "replacing." When you audio dub a video segment, you are totally erasing all of the sound and replacing it with new sound.

Here's an example of when you might use audio dub. Construction workers have just broken ground on a new gymnasium for your school, and you want to prepare a brief story for your news show. You have the basic facts—when construction will begin, how much it will cost, when it will be completed, and so on—but you don't have time to create a complex, edited segment. So you grab a camcorder and go take five or six shots of the cleared construction site. Maybe there are bulldozers clearing the land. Perhaps you could even include a few shots of students playing basketball on an outdoor court, rather than inside a nice gymnasium.

Back in the studio, you watch your videotape, time it, and write a script to supplement the video. You select some appropriate music for the segment (more on that later), and now you're ready to audio dub.

Realize that audio dub is a function on a VCR. Some VCRs have audio dub, and others do not. Until a few years ago, only the most expensive VCRs had this function. Now, many VCRs in the $100 price range have audio dub. Simply cue your videotape to the beginning of your video footage, press the audio dub button (this varies depending on the type of VCR you have), and you're ready to record new voice and music.

After you've finished the audio dub, just press stop, rewind, and recue, and you're ready to use the segment on your school news show.

Mixing Voice and Music

Audio mixing is an art—no doubt about it. A good audio technician demands a high salary in the TV studio because of his skill and experience. Mixing voice and music at the appropriate levels is an important skill. If the music is too loud, then the voice can't be heard. If the music is too soft, the audience won't be able to hear it. Here is an introduction to mixing voice and music for the beginner.

The first consideration is the microphone. As we learned in Chapter 2, a unidirectional microphone is great for a single-source speaker. An omnidirectional microphone could collect sounds from all around the studio. For a good announcing session, the microphone should be placed on a desk stand. Asking the announcer to hold the microphone will probably result in handling noises, and the announcer might not always maintain the proper distance from the microphone.

That proper distance is six-to-eight inches from the source. As an audio technician, it is your job to create an environment that will make this distance comfortable to the announcer. Don't expect your announcer to lean forward into the microphone.

Ask the announcer to speak into the microphone. Use your headphones and VU meters to make sure that the microphone is working properly. Any static in the sound indicates a problem with the microphone or microphone cable. These problems will not go away and will probably ruin your production. Select another microphone if you hear static in the line.

Set the output master on your audio mixer at about 75 percent. This will give you plenty of room to decrease the level, and some room to raise it if necessary.

Now have your announcer read the script in the same tone that he or she plans to use for the recording. Using "Testing . . . one . . . two . . . three" isn't very productive. It's better to set the levels by creating the actual recording situation. Adjust the microphone input so that the master output VU peaks at 100 percent. Use the trim to adjust the individual microphone input if needed.

Next play the music that you will use in this production. Start by setting the level at about half of the level of the microphone. Have the announcer read the script and make adjustments to the music level as needed.

Now that you have added music, the master level will probably be too high. If needed, turn it down so that the combination of narration and music peaks at 100% VU.

Let's do a quick rehearsal. Press record (or audio dub, if appropriate) on your recording device, start the music, and ask the announcer to read the first few lines of script. Listen using the headphones and adjust the levels as needed.

Now play the recording back through the TV. This is how your audience will probably hear the program (most television audiences don't wear headphones!). How does it sound? Do you need one more rehearsal?

Using Production Music

You will probably want to use music in many of your video production projects. However, you've probably also discovered that many of the songs in your personal collection just don't work very well in video production class. You've probably also heard about potential copyright problems that can arise from copying videotaped segments containing popular music or broadcasting those segments. Some school districts have specific policies about music use in schools, and others do not. The next few paragraphs describe a better alternative that avoids copyright problems—production music.

Professional Production Music

Production music is music created specifically for use in audio and video programs. When a school buys production music, they also buy copyright permissions not granted with standard music purchases. So students and teachers at the school can use this music in their video projects, make (and even sell) copies of the program, and broadcast the program without paying royalties and without fear of violating copyright law. When you buy production music, you're buying the right to do this. It's included in the price.

Production music is a bit more expensive than popular music. Schools can expect to pay $50 or more for a CD filled with production music. Fortunately, as a student that's not your problem. Every school should own and use several CDs of production music.

Avoiding copyright problems is one of the biggest reasons to buy and use production music, but there are several other reasons.

- Production music is anonymous. Probably no one has ever heard your music selection, and no one already has opinions or emotions connected to it. If you use a popular song, it may trigger unwanted memories or opinions from your audience members.

- Production music allows for theme building. Because production music is anonymous, you can select certain songs to be theme music for your shows and segments.

- Production music is created for narration. Production music almost never contains words and usually doesn't contain a dominant instrument playing a lead or melody line. Your announcer won't have to struggle against song lyrics or overpowering instruments.

- Production music has acceptable content. Let's face it—some of the music available today just isn't appropriate for school use. Production music is always "safe."

- Production music creates a professional atmosphere in your studio. As the audio technician, you can select from a library of music just like they use at a real television studio. Friends won't pressure you to play their favorite songs on the news show. The professionals use production music, and you should, too.

- Production music is available in various lengths. Typically, a production music song is presented on a CD in several lengths. The first song in Figure 3.14—a listing of tracks on a production music CD—is called "Momentum." Track 1 is a full version of "Momentum," just over four minutes long. Track 11 is a one-minute version of "Momentum"—great for program themes or longer commercials. Track numbers 21, 31, 41, 51, and 61 are shorter versions of "Momentum" that could be used for quick segues to commercials or segments. A typical production music CD has several versions of ten to fifteen tunes.

Track	Time	Title	:59	:29	:14	:06-:10	:03-:06	Logo (:10)
1	4:11	Momentum	11	21	31	41	51	61
2	3:31	Licked Clean	12	22	32	42	52	62
3	3:09	Precision Groove	13	23	33	43	53	63
4	4:45	Vision	14	24	34	44	54	64
5	3:15	Charlie's Caper	15	25	35	45	55	65
6	4:39	When Time Changed	16	26	36	46	56	66
7	3:54	Day In, Day Out	17	27	37	47	57	67
8	4:36	Motor Skills	18	28	38	48	58	68
9	3:29	Old Home Place	19	29	39	49	59	69
10	2:42	Vocality	20	30	40	50	60	70

The Corporate Series — **MIXDOWN**

A collection of corporate, industrial, blues, jazz, dixieland, techno, rock, country and new age.

Full Length Tracks — **Other Versions - Tracks 11 - 70**

Davenport Productions, PO Box 690536, Charlotte, NC 28227-7009
1-800-951-6666 • 704-535-4171 • Fax 704-535-4155
www.davenportmusic.com

℗© Copyright 2003 Davenport Productions
All Rights Reserved

Fig. 3.14. Production music track listing: note the various lengths of each song.

At this point, you might be thinking, "Oh no, elevator music." That might have been true some time ago, but it's not true now. Production music companies have realized that their customers want exciting, sophisticated songs just like those heard on the radio, and they have responded by creating some great production music. Give it a try, and if you don't find something you like, keep listening.

If your school doesn't have a collection of production music for you to use, encourage your instructor to make this valuable resource available to you. It's easy to investigate production music companies; they all have Web sites, and most of them have samples of their songs for download. A list of Web site addresses appears at the end of this chapter.

Making Your Own Production Music

Several software products allow you to create your own production music. There are two types of production music software: loops-based and SmartSound software.

Loops-Based Software

A music loop is a four- or eight-beat section of music played by one musical instrument. This brief musical segment is stored as a computer file and can be looped—played over and over again—in song form. When several loops are played at the same time, the result is a song. Because you created the song by sequencing the loops, you own the copyright. Loops-based music creation programs include Screenblast ACID® Music Mixing Software by Sony and Cakewalk for Windows operating systems and Garage Band and Soundtrack for the Mac. (Sony also makes Super Duper Music Looper® loops-based music creation software for the elementary school market.)

Creating a song can be as simple or complex as the song itself. Most music creators start with a drum loop, then add keyboards, bass, guitars, and maybe even horns and percussion instruments. Each loop is "painted" across the timeline. You can add or subtract loops throughout the song—you don't have to make all loops play all the time (Figure 3.15).

If you have a good ear, a little time, and you know which musical instruments sound good together, then you'll probably enjoy creating your own production music with a loops-based software program. If you're looking for a quicker solution or you feel more comfortable selecting from a menu of songs (rather than starting from scratch), then check out SmartSound Software.

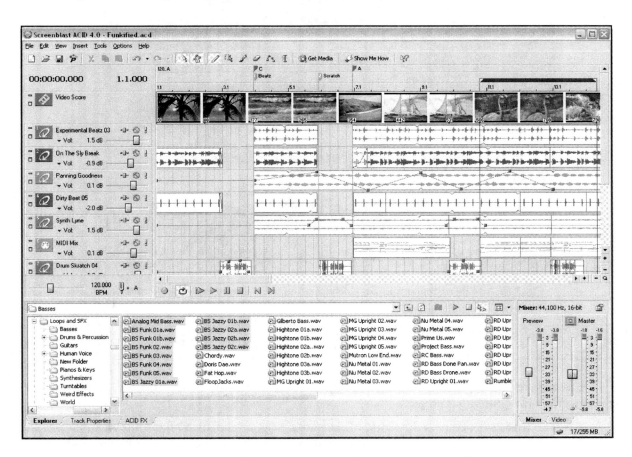

Fig. 3.15. Loops-based music production: Screenblast ACID®.

SmartSound Software

SmartSound Software (both Windows and Mac) lets you create custom production music from pre-made fully instrumented segments. A loop contains just one musical instrument. A SmartSound segment contains all of the instruments in that song. SmartSound software automatically combines these segments into several versions, and you can choose the version that best fits your project. Just tell the software what type of music you'd like (rock, pop, world music, etc.) and the program provides you with a list of choices. You can also dictate the exact length for your musical selection. SmartSound currently publishes two software products—Movie Maestro for the beginning and intermediate user (Figure 3.16), and SonicFire Pro, designed for the video professional. Web sites for all of these software titles are listed at the end of the chapter.

Fig. 3.16. Adding custom music to a video program using SmartSound Movie Maestro.

Scriptwriting Tips

We've referred to narration several times in this chapter. Before we end, here are a few tips on writing your scripts for your video projects.

- The first sentence tells the story. Make sure that your audience knows the main idea of the video project after the first few words. For example, "Construction crews began work yesterday on our new school gymnasium."

- Use the active voice whenever possible. Active voice means that the subject of your sentences is performing the action of the sentence. Here's an example of active voice: "The school board voted last year to award the construction contract to a local company." Here's the same idea, written in passive voice: "The contract was awarded by the school board to a local company." Just doesn't pack the same punch, does it?

- Use creative verbs. The math students "attack" their final exams. The football team "battles" a cross-town rival. The band "paraded" down the street.

- Don't headline. We're used to putting a title on our papers, like newspaper headlines—"Construction Begins on New Gymnasium"—but that's not a very good way to begin a news report. Make sure that all of your sentences are complete sentences.

- Use a "people" angle. People like to hear about other people. When possible, include the names of the people involved in the topic you're writing about. Remember, you might need to qualify those people by stating their relationship and importance to this story. For example, "School board member Stacey Smith," or "junior class president Albert Jones."

- Don't start sentences with "this is" or "here are." "This is the cafeteria." "This is the media center." "Here are the student council officers." Instead, use the previous script tips to devise more descriptive and creative sentences.

- Read the script aloud. Make sure that it makes sense to someone who doesn't know too much about your topic. After covering a story or creating a documentary, you might be an expert on the topic. Remember that the audience probably doesn't share your expertise.

A good script is another essential step in creating audio for your video productions. Take your time, be creative, and follow the suggestions listed here to make all of your scripts an outstanding component of your video projects.

Selected Manufacturer Web Sites

Audio Mixers

Behringer http://www.behringer.com
Mackie http://www.mackie.com
RadioShack http://www.radioshack.com

Music Creation Software

Apple Soundtrack http://www.apple.com/sountrack
Cakewalk http://www.cakewalk.com
Screenblast ACID® http://www.screenblast.com
SmartSound Software http://www.smartsound.com

Production Music

Davenport Music http://www.davenportmusic.com
Mokal Music http://www.productionmusicmall.com
Music2Hues http://www.music2hues.com
Signature Music http://www.sigmusic.com
PBTM/QCCS Music Library http://www.pbtm.com
Soundzabound Music Library http://www.soundzabound.com
The Canary Collection http://www.canarymusic.com
The Music Bakery http://musicbakery.com

Review Questions

1. What are the two types of inputs on an audio mixer?

2. Sound levels are usually controlled by fader bars and potentiometers ("pots"). What is the difference in the way these two controls are used?

3. In your own words, describe the difference between audio level and audio volume.

4. Name three possible destinations for the output of an audio mixer.

5. Why is trim an important feature for an audio mixer?

6. Name five possible audio input devices and give an example of how each can be used in the video production setting.

7. Name the three common connectors used in audio production.

8. Does an adapter change impedance? Why is this important to know?

9. What happens to the original sound on a videotape during the audio dub process?

10. Can every VCR perform an audio dub? Explain your answer.

11. Using production music in the video production setting allows us to avoid copyright problems. Name six additional reasons the use of production music is desirable.

12. Write a paragraph describing one of the scriptwriting tips listed at the end of the chapter. Include an example of what would happen if this tip were not taken seriously.

Student Project Plan

Audio Commercial

Description of Completed Project

The finished project will be a 30- to 45-second audio commercial, recorded on videotape.

Method

1. Write a script for an audio commercial. Your script should take 30 to 45 seconds to read at a comfortable pace. Make sure to use correct grammar. You might even want to type your script using a word processor and enlarge the font size to make it easier to read.

2. Select appropriate background music for your script. Make sure the music matches the mood of your commercial.

3. Practice reading your script.

4. Create a graphics screen on the character generator. Include the following information: announcer name (you), audio technician's name, date, class period, and client (the company sponsoring the commercial).

5. A fellow student will serve as your audio technician.

6. Roll videotape, and record the graphic with the audio.

7. You will also receive a grade based on your service as an audio technician for another student's audio project.

Evaluation

The completed project will be worth 100 points.

- Script (20 points)
- Graphics (10 points)
- Voice performance (20 points)
- Music selection (10 points)
- Audio technician (40 points)

Evaluation Sheet: Audio Commercial

NAME _____ DATE _____

Script . . . . (20 points) _____

Does the script engage the listener? Does the script accurately describe the product or service? Are the words easy to listen to?

Teacher Comments:

Graphics. . . . . (10 points) _____

Did you include all of the information requested? Is the spelling correct? Is the graphic easy to read?

Teacher Comments:

Voice Performance . . . . (20 points) _____

Is each word spoken clearly? Is the voice tone appropriate for the subject matter? Is the voice engaging?

Teacher Comments:

Music Selection . . . . (10 points) _____

Is this an appropriate musical selection for this commercial? Can the narration be heard? Does the mood of the music match the content of the script?

Teacher Comments:

Audio Technician . . . . (40 points) _____

Student announcer when you were audio technician _____

Are the microphone and music levels correctly mixed? Is the master level set at an appropriate level. Can we easily hear all parts of the program?

Teacher Comments:

Total Points . . . . (Out of 100) _____

Teacher Comments:

4 PROJECT PLANNING

Objectives

After successfully completing this chapter, you will be able to

- identify the elements of project planning.
- plan and strategize a video project.
- complete the elements of a script.
- complete the elements of a storyboard.
- organize the materials and resources needed to complete a video project.
- produce a documentary.

Vocabulary

audio. The portions of the video project that include sound (dialogue, music, or background sounds).

brainstorming. Creatively identifying and listing possible ideas and topics for a project.

character generator. A video component that allows the typing of words and simple graphics onto the video screen.

font. A letter type or style used in character generation.

script. The written portion of the video project that depicts the "spoken" part of the audio components.

storyboarding. The process of planning a video project that includes drawing a simple sketch of the desired shot, planning the accompanying audio, and estimating the duration of each element.

topic elements. The information, concepts, and ideas about the topic that are to be included in the video program.

If you truly want to be successful in video production, it is essential that you develop an understanding of the elements of project planning. Successful video projects are carefully planned, thoughtfully scripted, and then effectively produced. Beginning students are often frustrated with their initial attempts in video production because they have not been adequately planned and scripted before the production process has begun. Not only does this result in less-than-ideal finished products, but the process often is more time-consuming and less efficient for both personnel and resources. Careful project planning cannot always ensure avoiding the mistakes of the novice video production enthusiast, but it can help to minimize errors and make the process more enjoyable for all those involved.

Topic Selection

What makes a good topic for a video project? Generally, millions of topics abound in the world that surrounds us, but it is the video producer's creative and unique way of depicting the topic makes that topic worthwhile. A variety of topics and subjects of video projects abound in the school setting. Taking these ordinary topics and using a creative approach for them facilitates success and interest in your video project.

Brainstorming is an excellent way for you and your production crew to generate ideas for a video program. The process is easy and enlists the creative ideas and talents of a production group to identify a topic and approach for a video project. In the brainstorming session, the production crew (or writing team), will generate and submit ideas for topics. As each idea or topic is suggested, the ideas are written down on paper, a whiteboard, or even a computer. At first, no idea is discarded, and each is written down for later discussion. Within a few minutes, your group will compile a possible list of topics for the video program (Figure 4.1). Once a list has been compiled, ideas are discussed one by one within the group. Crewmembers should bring up both pros and cons for each topic for discussion and debate. During this debate, some suggested topics will be eliminated or discarded. The list can be narrowed down to one or two good ideas. During discussion, the production crew should consider the following aspects of each topic idea to see if that idea or topic is viable:

Fig. 4.1. Students share topic ideas during a brainstorming session.

1. *Is the idea feasible?* That is, does the crew have the ability (skills) and the resources (equipment) to produce the project?

2. *Are the time constraints realistic?* Can the project be produced within the time frame established for project completion?

3. *Is the topic politically and social acceptable?* Because this is an educational facility and classroom, you need to adhere to the values, morals, and standards expected in the school's student code of conduct and guidelines.

Discuss each topic your group has considered using these rationales. Narrow down the ideas to only those topics that are feasible, realistic, and appropriate for your school or program's objectives. Every member of the production crew should be able to contribute to the discussion during the brainstorming session, making the final topic choice a suitable one.

Identifying Topic Elements

After your topic has been successfully identified as both feasible and viable, it is now time to consider which elements of the topic to include in the video project. The scope of the project is often constrained by length and time. A 2-minute finished product would have many more limitations in terms of "what" can be covered than a 10-minute finished product. Defining the elements, or the scope of the project, is important in the planning process. Let's look at an example of identifying topic elements.

Identified Topic: Student parking at your school
Elements to be covered:

1. Number of students versus number of parking spaces

2. Application process for parking permits

3. Senior parking spaces: uniquely named "spaces"

4. Do's and Don'ts (parking rules)

5. Alternatives for those who cannot obtain parking privileges

Of course the number of elements that can be covered in this video project is constrained by the time limits associated with the finished program. If, for instance, the time limit for the video project is 2 minutes, perhaps only a few of the elements can be covered. A longer program, say 5 or 10 minutes, would be able to cover all the elements in the list. It is up to the production crew to determine which of these elements would be best to include in the video project. Identifying the key elements to be covered is important in the production planning process.

Topic Approaches

The "approach" or point of view you will take during the production of the topic is what makes the project unique and interesting to the viewer. Successful video producers can take a mundane and ordinary topic and employ a unique and creative approach in the production process to produce an extraordinary and interesting program. Enlist the creative talents and ideas of the production crew to identify some of the various approaches and situations that can be applied to project the elements of the topic to the viewer. Documentaries, commercials, public service announcements, and news reports all contain unique angles and strategies to capture the interest and attention of the viewer. Varying the way a topic is approached gives a fresh, new look to a worn-out subject.

Creative approaches can utilize unique camera angles, special effects, dazzling postproduction and editing, the appeal of good scriptwriting, or even on-camera talent personalities. Make use of the strengths and talents of the production crew to determine which approach to take and how to produce it. Again, let's consider the topic, "Student Parking at the School." Some unique ways to approach this topic might include:

- A *dramatization.* This approach takes a "movie-like" view on the subject. A student, Ryan, is the subject of the video and is followed through the process of trying to obtain a parking pass. He encounters a series of adventures and characters as he starts and completes the process.

- A *documentary.* This approach takes a serious look at some of the aspects of obtaining and using a parking pass. The script is narrated and includes background music as viewers watch and learn about the process of obtaining the pass and following some simple rules and regulations. The final scene interjects some comedy, as our subject (who has successfully obtained his pass) is seen circling the parking lot over and over trying to find an empty space after arriving to school late.

- A *news report*. This approach could be used in conjunction with the production of a school news program. A reporter is assigned to find out facts about the parking situation and process, interview administrators and students about the topic to get their viewpoints and opinions, and offer a variety of tips and suggestions for students to be successful in the process (Figure 4.2).

- A *commercial*. This approach uses humor to produce a commercial for the parking pass. Unique videography, narration, music, and graphics are all used to produce a one-minute commercial that creates interest and relays information about the process and privileges of using a school parking permit.

Fig. 4.2. News reports are a popular approach for school topics.

Using creativity within the brainstorming process can enhance the effectiveness and appeal of the video program. Identifying the topic and its elements leads to the development of ideas for inclusion in the video project. The approach to the topic can be unique and interesting, even if the topic idea is not.

Scriptwriting

After successfully identifying the topic and approach you will use, the next step in the planning process is writing the script. Whether you're planning a simple interview or a complicated documentary, the script comes first. That is a difficult concept for some students to grasp because when they think "video production," their first instinct is to grab a camera and make some tape. Shooting first and writing later results in a loss of valuable time. Not only will the production crewmembers videotape more footage than they need, they often leave out scenes and shots that are necessary for completion of the project. When they realize this, what will they do? Go out and shoot again. Writing the script first eliminates these problems.

A script can take many forms, depending on the approach you will use to cover the topic. If it is a news report about the topic, the script will include a reporter lead-in, some narration, a few questions for on-camera guests and interviews, and possibly a summary of the information presented during the report. A documentary, on the other hand, will include a more comprehensive script that includes background and relevant facts, information for the viewer, observations, and maybe some on-camera segments. A dramatization, with scenes and character portrayal, would include not only dialogue, but stage directions and emotional direction as well. A commercial or public service announcement can be as simple as writing a paragraph or as detailed as a dramatization, depending on the approach and production of the topic. Again, let's take our example of "Student Parking at the School" and look at some brief sample scripts based on the approaches we have described.

Script Sample: School Parking Passes (Dramatization)

In a dramatization script, settings, dialogue, and direction cues are included.

Scene 1. (*Inside Ryan's house, early morning. Ryan is packing his book bag for the first day of school*)

Mother (*Voice off camera*): Ryan, you better hurry up or you'll miss the bus. You don't want to be late on your first day of school.

Ryan: I'm not riding the big yellow cheese-wagon. I'm taking my car!

Mother: Oh . . . did you get a parking pass. I reminded you about that every day the last two weeks and you never—

Ryan (*Interrupting her as he runs out the door*): Don't worry 'bout it! I'm covered! (*Door slams*)

Script Sample: School Parking Passes (Documentary)

A documentary script is written in a narrative style. It may also contain some elements in which talent or guests appear on camera.

"Each school day, thousands of students and hundreds of cars compete for parking at North Lake High School. What separates those who can park from those that can't? The school's parking permit! With only 500 registered available spaces, administrators have provided a process and a privilege for those determined to drive their cars on campus. Unlicensed vehicles are turned away at the gate."

(*Insert shot of security officer speaking about turning away vehicles without passes here*)

"If you don't want to be one of those unfortunate students turned away at the gates, the process of obtaining a parking pass is as easy as remembering the combination of your locker."

Script Sample: School Parking Passes (A News Report)

A script for a news report should contain reporter on-camera statements, questions to be posed to on-camera guests, and possibly some narrative to be used for voice-overs.

Reporter (*On camera, standing in parking lot*): This year there are more than 1,200 juniors and seniors at North Lake High School. However, there are only 500 student parking spaces available. Can you do the math?

Questions for students with parking passes:

1. How valuable is your parking pass?

2. What motivated you to come to school this summer to get a parking pass?

Questions for administrators:

1. What were some of the criteria for selecting applicants for parking passes this year?

2. What can students do now who don't have parking passes and still want to obtain one?

Reporter Narration (*Off camera, voice-over*): According to administrators, a new section of parking under construction will be available after the first semester. Students are advised to obtain applications now for these valuable spaces.

Script Sample: School Parking Passes (PSA)

"Stacia has a radical vehicle . . . it's got leather seats . . . mag wheels . . . kicking bass sounds . . . tinted windows . . . neon lights . . . a 350-V8 engine . . . and even more important—A PARKING PASS!"

Successful scriptwriting is a key to successful video production. What you say and how you say it is just as important as the images you portray on the screen. Exhilarating videography loses its appeal when the script is drab and boring. Special effects and dazzling postproduction cannot rectify a poorly written narrative. Some simple suggestions for writing your scripts include the following:

• Write down ideas first! Perhaps a few good phrases or creative dialogue.

• Write for your audience. If the video project is designed to be shown to students, use words and language that they understand and relate to. If you are producing a project that will be shown to adults (even a contest video), language and syntax should be more structured.

- The tone should reflect the content. Video projects about sports events, school carnivals, and fun extracurricular activities should be written to make them seem exciting and entertaining. A video project about the effects of smoking would take a more serious tone and include important facts and research.

- It is important to identify titles and names of people in your project. Don't expect the viewer to know them just because you do. Graphics can also be used for this purpose. (More on this in the section about character generators.)

Incorrect: Mr. Rudzik will be presenting information at tonight's parent meeting.

Correct: North Lake's principal, Mr. Rudzik, will be presenting information at tonight's parent meeting.

- Use a "people" angle. People like to hear about themselves and people they know.

Incorrect: The ninth-grade students won several awards at this year's Student Poetry Festival.

Correct: Ms. Savoldi's ninth-grade English students won several awards at this year's Student Poetry Festival. Christopher Ryan and Sarah Keith both took first place honors.

- Don't be afraid to revise and rewrite. First drafts are good, second and third revisions are usually better.

- Let other crew members, teachers, or friends read your script. They can often provide additional help, creativity, or find flaws that you overlooked.

Scriptwriting is a skill that can be developed and cultivated with energy, enthusiasm, and practice. Successful scriptwriting is one of the key components in video project planning (Figure 4.3).

Fig. 4.3. Students collaborate during a scriptwriting session.

Storyboarding

After completion of the script, the next step in the planning process is to begin storyboarding the video project. Storyboarding is the process of planning a video production by drawing a simple sketch of the desired video shot, writing an audio portion (or description of the audio if not scripted), and listing an approximate time for the sequence. Storyboarding is an important part of the production process. By using a storyboard to design a project on paper before starting the production process, you can avoid making costly and time-consuming mistakes on camera.

A storyboard is a printed outline of what the completed video project will look like. There are three components in a storyboard: video, audio, and the estimated time of each camera shot (see Figure 4.4). Storyboarding is a task best performed by one individual or a small group. Certain scenes can be assigned to individuals or groups, thus allowing for continuity within the scenes. Whether or not they realize it, videographers develop a certain style in their video production. Do you use a moving camera, or a tripod? Are the preferred camera angles close-ups, extreme close-ups, unstable horizon shots, or bust and medium shots? The completed storyboard will reflect your production and shooting style.

Storyboard

Project _____ **Page**_____ **of**_____

Visual	Audio	Time
_____ _____		_____ _____
_____ _____		_____ _____
_____ _____		_____ _____

Fig. 4.4. A storyboard includes three components: video, audio, and the estimated time of each camera shot.

Storyboarding a dramatization or documentary is somewhat more difficult than, say, storyboarding a news report. Depending on your editing capabilities, any and all scenes in your project could include many different shots and camera angles. Try to include as many camera angles and shot sequences as possible without detracting from your script.

It is easier to proceed through the process of storyboarding if the audio section is completed first. If you know what the talent will say in the video, it is easier to visualize the camera angle and shot composition to use for that sequence. A quick way to accomplish this task is to type the script on a computer and format the paper to coincide with the storyboard frames, using a small font and narrow margins. It then becomes a simple task to print out the script and cut and paste it within the storyboard frames. Some production teams actually have their storyboard forms already saved on a computer file and simply type in the corresponding script and then print them out in their completed form. It is also important to include references to background audio components as well. This might include music, sound effects, or ambient background sounds.

The visual aspect, or camera angles, of the storyboard can be somewhat more difficult to complete for beginning producers. If your drawing ability is not adept enough to clearly indicate exactly what the camera shots and angles are, it is also helpful to include a brief written description in the frame as well. Usually within a production class, several students have some talent with sketching or drawing the camera angles. If not, perhaps the production crew could enlist assistance from the art program to complete the storyboards. TV production members could add the audio components, and the art students could work in conjunction with them by completing the drawings.

The final aspect of the storyboard, the time sequences, are used to assist in the production and editing of the scenes. They also give the production crew a reliable estimate of the total length of the completed video program. It is helpful, for example, if you storyboard a shot of a car being driven by a student so that the videographer and the editor know how long that sequence will be in the completed video program. The first frame of the video project will start with a time of 00:00 and end with the time that indicates the length of the camera shot. A six-second shot will start at 00:00 and end at 00:06. The next frame begins at 00:06 and the end time of that frame will be indicated by the length of that camera angle. The completed storyboard will indicate not only the length of each shot, but also the completed time of the entire project

Figure 4.5 is an example of a partial storyboard for the "dramatization" video project about the student parking passes that will help you visualize how the video, audio, and time components are used in a production.

Production Team: Crew #1

Topic: Student Parking Passes (Dramatization)

Video Shot/Description	Audio (Script and sound)	Time (0:00)
 Medium shot of Ryan packing his book bag with folders and notebooks	*Mother's Voice (Off-camera)* Ryan, you better hurry up or you'll miss the bus. You don't want to be late for your first day of school!	00:00 00:06
 Bust shot of Ryan looking upstairs	I'm not riding the big yellow cheese-wagon. I'm taking my car!	00:06 00:11
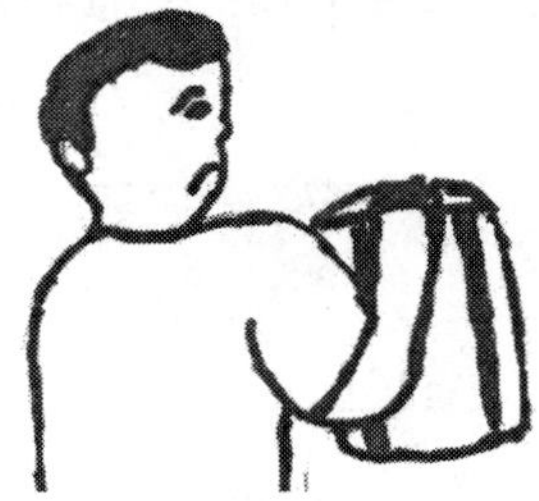 Over the shoulder shot of Ryan zipping bag and looking irritated.	*Mother's Voice (Off Camera)* Oh…did you finally get a parking pass. I reminded you about that every day the last two weeks and you never…..	00:11 00:17
 Low angle shot, walks past camera out door.	Don't worry 'bout it, I got it covered!! *(Door slam)*	00:17 00:22

Fig. 4.5. Storyboard example.

This storyboard example illustrates how a video project is planned, written, and designed on paper before the production process begins. Storyboard creation is a skill that improves with practice and experience. If you follow the simple advice that follows, you'll find that your early storyboarding attempts will be successful.

1. Keep it simple. Even if you are aspiring artists, stick to simple drawings. Storyboards are used to remind the producers of video shots and composition. Minor details aren't important.

2. Draw the actual shot. If you want a close-up, draw a close-up. Imagine how the shot would look if you were watching it on TV.

3. Consider point of view. What angle or shot best represents how the character is viewed in the shot? What angles will have an impact on the viewer?

4. Use the margins or frames for notes. You can write notes about the selected shots to give the videographers more information that can compensate for less talented storyboard artists.

5. Estimate the length of each shot. Not only will this give you an idea of how long your project will be, it also reminds the videographer of how long to tape each scene. Beginning videographers tend to have quick "trigger" fingers and wind up taping only a few seconds of footage when they might need 10 to 12 seconds.

6. Use arrows to indicate panning, tilt, or zoom motions for the camera, or even for talent notes. Perhaps your reporter is going to walk into the scene. You can indicate that by using an arrow for directional notes.

7. Don't forget to storyboard all aspects of your project: video shots, graphics, audio (including music and sound effects). Having a complete and concise storyboard means your crew will be better prepared for production and postproduction.

The time spent in storyboarding will pay off big dividends in production. Students will be more organized and confident in the outcome of their production efforts. Careful storyboarding, knowledge of the various camera angles used in video, and creative scriptwriting can make your video projects more informative and entertaining.

Graphics

Electronic character generation is used in almost every type of video production. Documentaries, movies, commercials, and even ENG (electronic news gathering) reports now include titles, credits, and internal graphics describing the task, content, or even on-camera appearances of talent and guests. Recent developments in electronic and computer technology have made character generation easily affordable and accessible to school video production departments. Stand-alone character generators are available from a variety of consumer and professional electronic vendors (Figure 4.6). This moderately priced technology offers a wide range of features (fonts, colors, backgrounds, effects) for use in school video production activities. Today's generation of character generators can easily be configured into existing video and editing systems. Stand-alone character generators can also be connected to VCR and DVD recorders for the recording of graphic screens to be later used in video production activities.

Fig. 4.6. A character generator: Videonics Titlemaker 3000.

Computer-based graphic programs can also be used for creating graphics in video production programs. Title and graphic screens are transferred to videotape or other recordable media via the computer's video output jack or by using a conversion device to convert the computer signals (VGA) into video signals (VHS, SVHS).

The vast array of nonlinear editing systems available today also offer an internal source for creating graphics during postproduction. A wide variety of fonts, transitions, and screen backgrounds can be used to create graphics during the postproduction process (Figure 4.7).

Successful character generation, like scriptwriting, is a craft and an art. The best graphics grab the audience's attention and convey information nonverbally in a brief time. Whether you are making a simple title screen for your project or detailing important information for the viewer, there are some important guidelines to follow so you can communicate effectively with the viewer.

Fig. 4.7. Nonlinear editing systems provide access to graphics and titles during postproduction.

- Be aware of character size as it relates to the viewing situation. If you are preparing graphics for broadcast television, you can use smaller sizes than if you are producing a program to be seen in a classroom from a distance of 20 feet. The graphics for the latter need to be large so they can be read from a distance.

- Use a variety of fonts. If your character generator is capable of producing various types sizes and letter fonts, learn to use them in your programs. Your audience will respond favorably to several fonts and colors on a screen.

- Use high-contrast colors and shades. A dark font color on a light background or a light colored font on a dark background will be easier for the viewer to read and decipher. Avoid using light pastel colors for fonts because these have a tendency to dissipate when broadcast or duplicated.

- When you are using a transparent background, be aware of the contrast between the background video footage and the color of the letter font. Using an outline color for the lettering can also assist in creating graphics and titles that stand out from the video footage.

- Don't overcrowd a page. Three pages of graphics with two or three lines each will communicate information more effectively than one page with nine lines. After reading two or three lines, the audience will tire or give up (Figure 4.8).

- Keep it simple. Your audience is prepared to watch a program, not read a book. Use graphics and characters to accent your video, not replace it.

- Spelling is important! Carefully proofread your graphics for spelling and grammatical errors.

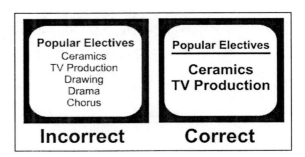

Fig. 4.8. Examples of incorrect and corrected graphic screens.

If you are planning on using graphics in your video program during postproduction, it is wise to include them in the video frames of your storyboard.

A helpful hint: Type or print the graphics you will be using on index cards for production or preproduction activities. This saves time and reduces errors when graphics are hastily added during the postproduction phases of your program.

Success in video production can always be traced back to planning. Activities such as writing scripts, planning introductions and questions for guests, and organizing storyboards always lead to success on a project. You will be successful if you employ these aspects of video production before you turn on the cameras, microphones, and editing devices.

Review Questions

1. Describe the process of brainstorming and how it relates to topic selection.

2. List and describe the three criteria used to determine whether a topic is appropriate for a video production activity.

3. Identify three topic elements that could be included in the following video projects:

    1. School dress code policy

    2. Teacher shortages in your state

    3. Balancing schoolwork and after-school jobs

4. List and describe two approaches you could use to produce a program called "Preparing for the SATs."

5. List and describe three important tips or techniques for successful scriptwriting.

6. What is a storyboard? What three important elements does a storyboard include?

7. List three advantages of creating a storyboard *before* beginning production on your program.

8. What is a character generator?

9. Give three examples of how a character generator can be used in a video project.

10. In what sequence should the following planning activities take place? (Number from 1 to 6)

    Storyboarding _____   Topic selection_____

    Brainstorming _____   Identify topic elements_____

    Scriptwriting _____   Production_____

Student Project Plan: Documentary

Description of Completed Project

The finished project will be a two- to three-minute documentary on some facet of school or life at school. It may include video shots with narrative, on-camera talent and stand-ups (talent appears on camera), or opinions and comments by guests about the topic. Graphics in the project can include (but are not limited to) title screen and ending credits.

Method

1. Students will form production teams to work on project.

2. Production teams submit topic for teacher approval.

3. Production teams will create a script for the project and submit to teacher for approval.

4. Production teams will create a storyboard and submit to teacher for approval.

5. Production team will create graphics for use in the project.

6. Production team will complete necessary videography.

7. Production team will add narration, titles, and music (optional) to the finished documentary.

8. Production team will submit completed project for grading.

Evaluation

This completed project will be worth 200 points.

- Concept and storyboard (40 points)
- Titles and graphics (40 points)
- Videography (40 points)
- Narration/audio track (40 points)
- Overall production (40 points)

Evaluation Sheet: Documentary

Team Members _____

_____

Concept and Storyboard

Project topic . . . . (10 points) _____

Storyboard video . . . . (10 points) _____

Storyboard audio . . . . (10 points) _____

Completion . . . . (10 points) _____

Camera Work

Shot selection . . . . (10 points) _____

Shot composition. . . . . . . (10 points) _____

Shot lengths. . . . . (10 points) _____

Steady/focus . . . . (10 points) _____

Graphics/Titles

Contrast . . . . (10 points) _____

Spelling . . . . (10 points) _____

Fonts/sizes . . . . (10 points) _____

Page layout . . . . (10 points) _____

Audio

Volume (voice/music) . . . (20 points) _____

Voice talent . . . . (20 points) _____

Overall Production

Elements of topic appropriately covered . . . . (10 points) _____

Topic Approach . . . . (10 points) _____

Audience Appeal . . . . (10 points) _____

Postproduction . . . . (10 points) _____

Teacher Comments:

Total Points . . . . (Out of 200) _____

Student Project Plan: Commercial

Description of Completed Project

The finished project will be a 30- to 60-second commercial about a product or service offered at the school. The finished project must include video shots, graphics, and a soundtrack (voice, music, or both).

Method

1. Students will form production teams. Team size will vary depending on the scope of the project.

2. Production teams submit topic for teacher approval.

3. Production teams will create a script for the project and submit to teacher for approval.

4. Production teams will create a storyboard and submit to teacher for approval.

5. Production team will create graphics for use in the project.

6. Production team will complete necessary videography.

7. Production team will add narration, titles, and music (optional) to the finished documentary.

8. Production team will submit completed project for grading.

Evaluation

This completed project will be worth 200 points.

- Concept and Storyboard (40 points)
- Titles and Graphics (40 points)
- Videography (40 points)
- Narration/Audio Track (40 points)
- Overall Production (40 points)

Evaluation Sheet: Commercial

Team Members _____

_____

Concept and Storyboard

Project topic . . . . (10 points) _____

Storyboard video. . . . . . (10 points) _____

Storyboard audio. . . . . . (10 points) _____

Completion . . . . (10 points) _____

Camera Work

Shot selection . . . . (10 points) _____

Shot composition. . . . . . (10 points) _____

Shot lengths. . . . . (10 points) _____

Steady/focus . . . . (10 points) _____

Graphics/Titles

Contrast. . . . . (10 points) _____

Spelling . . . . (10 points) _____

Fonts/sizes. . . . . (10 points) _____

Page layout . . . . (10 points) _____

Audio

Volume (voice/music). . . (20 points) _____

Voice talent . . . . (20 points) _____

Overall Production

Elements of topic appropriately covered . . . . . (10 points) _____

Topic Approach. . . . . (10 points) _____

Audience Appeal . . . . (10 points) _____

Postproduction. . . . . (10 points) _____

Teacher Comments:

Total Points Awarded . . . . (Out of 200) _____

5 ELECTRONIC NEWS GATHERING

Objectives

After successfully completing this lesson, you will be able to

- List and describe the equipment needed to complete an electronic news gathering (ENG) report.
- Identify the videographer tasks necessary for producing ENG reports.
- Identify the reporter tasks necessary for producing ENG reports.
- Write scripts for ENG reports.
- Record an ENG report.
- Produce an ENG report.

Vocabulary

ENG. Electronic news gathering. Refers to the process of reporting events and activities that occur outside of the television studio.

lead-in. The first few sentences of script that establish the setting and events of a news story. Introduces the ENG topic to the viewer.

Rule of Threes. During postproduction, the edited clips are grouped by audio and video into segments of three sentences per style or format.

sound bite. A videotaped segment in which the audio and video portions of the tape must remain in sync. Sound bites are usually three to five seconds in length.

stand-up. Refers to an on-camera shot of a reporter as he or she presents information about the topic.

tag. A standard format for the final sentence of script ending an ENG report. Identifies the reporter (by name) and station affiliation.

ENG reporting is the cornerstone of any news show. Recording and reporting events and activities as they happen is what news is all about. The essence of electronic news gathering is "getting the story" and presenting this information to the viewer. Vital to the success of the report, the reporter and videographer need to work together to capture the drama, actions, emotions, and information and convey them to the viewer in an interesting and informative manner. The ENG reporter must quickly ascertain what is important about the activity and how it affects the participants and viewers (Figure 5.1). The videographer works closely with the reporter making sure the necessary video segments are recorded to coincide with the script and information. Successful ENG reporting requires both on-camera and behind-the-camera skills. Reproducing the excitement and energy of an event on videotape for broadcasting purposes is a skill: it requires expertise and training. Professional reporters spend many hours writing and revising scripts, interviewing people both on and off camera, researching topics, and critiquing their stories, as well as other professional broadcaster's work. Professional videographers perfect their craft through training and education, practice, as well as collaboration with other professionals in the field. A successful ENG team produces a video segment that enables viewers to experience the event as if they were there. Sights, sounds, and information are combined to provide news and entertainment for the viewing audience. They can vicariously experience an event, be entertained and informed, and form their own opinions, based on what they see and hear from an ENG report. What most people know about their world, fellow citizens, government, and social and political issues comes from TV. ENG reporting crews provide a powerful tool for disseminating information and experiences to the viewing public.

Fig. 5.1. An ENG reporter "at the scene."

ENG Equipment

In ENG reporting, there's no going back to the studio for equipment. The reporter and videographer must be prepared for every situation that might present itself during the reporting of an event. Larger television news stations have remote broadcast trucks and vans that they can send to locations to record and produce news segments at the scene. These are routinely outfitted so that they can remotely broadcast live from the scene via satellite and digital broadcast equipment. Many of these remote broadcast vehicles come equipped with editing equipment as well, so story segments can be produced and broadcast back to the studio during the production of a news program.

In the school setting, the necessary video and audio equipment needs to be carefully checked, packed, and transported to the location. Camcorder and batteries, microphones and cables, tapes, and even lights must be ready, working, and accessible when the ENG team arrives on the scene. Professional equipment bags and trunks should be purchased for transporting expensive video and audio equipment to locations (Figure 5.2).

Fig. 5.2. An ENG production team checks and packs equipment.

To avoid potential problems and catastrophes at the scene, a few minutes of consideration and preparation are needed. Some suggestions include the following:

1. Always check the camcorder and recording equipment before leaving the studio for taping. Turn on the camcorder and record a few seconds of footage. A simple playback will enable you to see whether it is working properly.

2. Microphones are essential for ENG reporting. You might need several types: handheld for interviews, lavaliere for reporter script, and even a shotgun for obtaining sound bites of distant activities.

3. Connect the microphone(s) and mic cords as well. A simple sound check with the camcorder or audio system will ensure they are working.

4. Bring several power sources. Besides a few extra (charged) batteries, it is wise to bring an AC power supply and battery charger.

5. Don't forget the essentials: videotapes, tripod, and headphones.

6. What about lighting? If you think you might need it, bring it.

7. A clipboard, notepad, and pen or pencil should be packed as well. Reporter notes and script as well as information, names (spelled correctly), and titles need to be written down for postproduction.

An ENG equipment checklist can be a viable tool to use for ensuring that all the necessary equipment is carefully packed and ready for transport. Reporters and videographers can determine what equipment they will need and then check it off as it is checked and packed. This checklist can also be used when returning to the studio to double-check that all of the equipment has been brought back and is in good working order (Figure 5.3).

Getting the Story

What topics or events should be covered by ENG news teams? Most television stations have an assignment editor who works with and directs ENG crews and assignments. Assignment editors are familiar with the television studio and equipment, as well as aware of the news programs and community and world events the station feels are newsworthy to the viewing audience. They are tuned into local news as it is happening by reading newspapers, listening to radio news coverage, monitoring police activity, and receiving tips from local organizations and their members about upcoming events. Once an event has been deemed newsworthy, a crew is assigned to cover and report the story.

In the school setting, ENG news events are generated by events and activities in which students, teachers, parents, and school athletes or artists are involved. Information about these events can be obtained by reading the school newspaper, talking to club and event sponsors, by listening to school announcements on the intercom or school news broadcast, or by creatively examining national and world events and how they relate to the student population.

Once an ENG topic has been defined, some preliminary research can be done. It is now time to find out the who, what, where, when, how, and why of the event. Researching the topic can take several forms. Telephone calls can be made to event organizers to get essential background information, as well as the times, dates, and locations of events. Face-to-face informal meetings with event organizers can also be arranged if organizers are located at the school or studio facility. Organizers can provide the ENG team with event background information (prior event history, attendance, purpose, schedule) as well as information about the event they would like to relay to the viewers (location, ticket prices, results).

ENG EQUIPMENT CHECKLIST

Videographer _____

Reporter _____

Event/Location _____

_____

Date _____

Item	Needed?	Checked Out	Returned
Camcorder			
Batteries			
AC Power/Charge			
Videotapes			
Tripod			
Microphone—handheld			
Microphone—lavaliere			
Microphone—shotgun			
Microphone—other			
Headphones			
Lighting			
Clipboard/Paper/Pen			
Other			

Fig. 5.3. An ENG equipment checklist.

Some topics may require using public or school library resources or the Internet for statistical and data information. For example, if one of your school's clubs is sponsoring an event to heighten awareness about teen drinking and driving, it would be beneficial to find out how many teen drivers were involved in drinking and driving accidents this past year either in your state or nationally (Figure 5.4). Background research is essential for many topics an ENG team will cover, especially social and political issues. This information can be used to formalize a preliminary script for the event.

Fig. 5.4. Students use the Internet to find important background information.

Once the ENG crew has arrived at the scene, each member has specific tasks to perform. While the videographer is concerned primarily with setting up the video and audio equipment, the reporter should begin to engage in preparing script and organizing guests for interviews or comments on camera. The reporter should quickly ascertain what is happening at the scene, what activities are planned, who is in charge, and obtain any current information about the event. A small notebook or clipboard should be used to write down relevant facts and information necessary for the report (Figure 5.5).

Here's an example of how a typical ENG crew would cover an assignment: A reporter and videographer have been assigned to report on the International Dinner and Dance sponsored by the school's foreign language department. Upon arriving, the reporter should complete the following tasks:

1. Locate a foreign language teacher or organizer connected with the event. Ask about event details: number of students involved, what activities are included, how the profits from the event will be used, and expected outcomes from the event.

Fig. 5.5. An ENG crew begins production at the scene.

2. Talk with several students involved in the project. Find out if they would be willing to talk on camera about the activity. Be sure to have an idea (a list would be great!) about the questions you will ask them. Write down their names (first, last) and how they are spelled, as well as any other information you may want to use in postproduction (e.g., foreign language class in which they are enrolled, grade level).

3. Begin to prepare your script. This should include a lead-in, possibly some narration to use with video images, and some questions you may wish to ask your guests on camera.

While the reporter is involved in his or her preliminary activities, the videographer should be completing the following ENG tasks:

1. Immediately set up and check the camcorder. Load the videotape, set up the tripod, and check the microphones.

2. Start videotaping some of the activities that are going on at the time: students and parents arriving for the dinner and dance, banners and hall decorations, food preparations, social interactions among guests (talking, dancing, laughing).

3. Spend some time with the reporter discussing camera shots and subject matter for the report. Verify shots and locations, as well as times, for the reporter stand-ups and interviews.

This example illustrates how each production crewmember has individual as well as team responsibilities for the ENG report. The reporter and videographer work together as a team to record and report, quickly and accurately, the events and activities.

Recording the Story

A good videographer will develop an eye for shots and angles that effectively capture the actions and emotions of an event. While the reporter is concerned with "telling" the story, the videographer must be concerned with recording the story in images and sound. This does not mean that every minute of the event, and hours and hours of videotape, must be recorded. Rather, the videographer should record several minutes of each activity as it occurs. A variety of camera shots and angles can be used so the most effective angle can be edited into the report during postproduction. Note that often the reactions and comments of people watching the activity are more interesting than the activity itself.

Camera angles and shots should reflect the atmosphere and mood of the event. Facial expressions and emotions of the people involved can be effectively recorded on tape and conveyed to your viewers. Close-ups and camera angles that bring the viewer into the action (over-the-shoulder shots, point-of-view angles) create interest in your report for the audience. They want to, and should, feel as if "they are there."

Sounds of the event are also an important element of every story and can be used effectively during postproduction to re-create the mood of the event. If the videographer consistently records only brief seconds of tape at a time, starting and stopping the camcorder after a few seconds, the soundtrack will be choppy and practically unusable for postproduction. A good videographer will effectively record and use sound, as well as video, for producing an ENG segment. The dinner dance, for example, would contain a multitude of sounds that could be used effectively in postproduction: international songs, students engaged in conversation in foreign languages, and perhaps some multicultural presentations and speeches. These sounds can be used as a background for reporter narration or video sequences.

"Sound bites," segments of the recorded tape in which both the audio and video will be used intact (as is) during postproduction, can be used to convey the sights and sounds of the event to your audience. The audience members "see" and "hear" the event as if they were there in person. In postproduction, sound bites can be used to separate the various components of the ENG report. For example, maybe your report begins with the reporter doing a stand-up. Then you can edit a short, two- to three-second sound bite from your clips, then move on to an interview or another reporter narration. Often an effective ENG report will begin with a good sound bite, which captures the viewer's attention and interest.

Comments from participants and guests are also an important aspect of recording the story. The videographer will be called on quite frequently to record these comments during the course of the activity.

Fig. 5.6. An example of a "talking head" shot with titles and graphics.

Most ENG news reports contain what are called "talking heads." That is, bust shots of people giving comments and opinions about the event or activity (Figure 5.6). The reporter is not seen on camera, and sometimes the question is not heard, but only the guest's responses. These types of shots are commonly used for ENG reports. A professional videographer needs to develop camera skills and techniques for recording these "talking heads."

Some guests will be interviewed by the reporter, and both the reporter and guest are seen on camera (Figure 5.7). One or more questions will be asked by the reporter and answered by the guest. During postproduction, editors can choose to select the whole interview or maybe just a part of it for use in the ENG report.

Some important considerations for recording comments and interviews from guests include the following:

1. Roll tape! Start recording even as the reporter and guests are getting set for the interview or comments on camera. Doing so eliminates color bars and control track problems on the tape, as well as providing adequate editing points for postproduction activities. It also eliminates the common novice mistake of "cutting off" the first few words at the beginning of the interview or comments. Continue to roll tape throughout the interview, even if mistakes are made and the reporter has to start anew. Let the tape roll for at least 15 to 20 seconds after the completion of the interview to eliminate the possibility of lost footage because of camcorder "roll back" or instant review of the interview at the scene.

2. Always wear headphones connected to the camcorder when recording interviews, comments, or reporter stand-ups and narration. This enables the videographer to hear the sound volume and quality while taping occurs and during playback (Figure 5.8).

3. Choose a good location for your interviews and comments. The background for the interview can enhance, or in other cases distract, from the interview itself. Beware of background lighting. Remember, the subject of the camera shot should be the brightest part of the picture. Avoid shooting into windows or sunlit objects, thereby making your subjects appear dark and shadowed (Figures 5.9 and 5.10).

4. Record reporter's stand-ups and narrations "at the scene" using the same microphone(s) used for the rest of the ENG report. Background noise will convey realism to the report that studio and postproduction narrations do not have.

Fig. 5.7. A typical interview with reporter and guest on camera.

Fig. 5.8. A videographer wears headphones to monitor sound during production.

Fig. 5.9. Example of a bad background for reporter.

Fig. 5.10. Example of a good background for reporter.

An ENG reporter and videographer will work together as a team coordinating their activities and developing style for their reports. Spend time together discussing both the video and audio aspects of the report and some creative techniques to get your points across.

Telling the Story

It is the reporter's task to tell the story that surrounds each event. The lead-ins and narratives should be informative, accurate, and brief. Present the information in a professional and unbiased manner. Do not editorialize! The purpose of the report is to present all the information the viewer needs to make his or her own judgments. Remember, every issue has two sides. Opinions do not belong in ENG reporting—well, at least not the reporter's opinions. If your subject is controversial or has both a pro and a con, use interviews and "talking heads" of guests to convey those opinions, not the reporter's stand-ups or narrations.

Reporter Lead-Ins

The reporter's lead-in is essential for informing the viewing audience about the topic. Lead-ins should be limited to two or three sentences that enable the viewer to quickly grasp the content of the report.

Incorrect: "As you can see, everyone here is having a good time. We have students and teachers dancing and eating."

(The reporter gives no information about the event.)

Correct: "The foreign language teachers and students are enjoying their Third Annual International Dinner and Dance. Local ethnic restaurants have donated their time and food to create an international menu fit for any five-star hotel. Funds from this event will be used to pay for field trips and guest speakers for foreign language classes this school year."

(The reporter gives good information, including the number of years the event has taken place and details about who participated in it and how the proceeds will be used.)

Not all ENG reports begin with a shot of the reporter, standing with mic in hand doing a lead-in. Although this is a common practice, there are several creative ways to begin your ENG report:

- Use a sound bite to begin your report. In this case, maybe a two- to three-second shot of someone serving a delicious plate of food and offering a "Bon Appetite" to a guest seated at a table.

- Start your ENG report with a POV (point of view) shot, such as a guest walking into a ballroom filled with music, dancing, and dining.

- Begin the report with a sequence of shots and use the reporter's lead-in as a narration. The viewers hear the reporter but see the video clips.

Reporter Narration

Almost all ENG reports contain some information that is generally narrated within the report, usually overlaid with video clips. To make this narration and maintain continuity with the rest of the project (sound quality, timbre sound characteristic, and tone), record the script while at the location during the event. You can record this with the reporter on or off camera, but use the camcorder and microphone to record the narration at the scene. This maintains a consistent sound quality throughout the audio portion of the edited project and preserves the ambience of the event on tape. The reporter and videographer should set a time during the event to record all narration from the script at one time. You can even do two or three "takes" of each section and choose the one during postproduction that you think is best.

Narration sequences, like lead-ins, should be limited to two or three sentences. Do not be too wordy. Remember, the audience will be "seeing" what you are talking about, and a picture is worth a thousand words. The reporter should speak clearly and distinctly and at a slightly slower rate than normal conversation. Again, your audience is "listening" for information, not having a conversation with you. Be animated, excited, and enthusiastic, but make sure your tone reflects the mood of the event. The International Dinner and Dance is going to have a different atmosphere than an SAT prep session on Saturday or a state swimming meet. The reporter's tone should reflect the tone of the event.

Interviews and Comments

One of the best ways to get and convey information is from the actual people involved in the event. Viewers, especially in a school setting, also like to see and hear about events from the people involved because they know them. It creates more interest in your report and gives credible information as well.

During an interview, the reporter may ask several questions of the guest. The questions should be open-ended (that is, questions that cannot be answered in just one or two words). Limit yourself to two or three questions.

Incorrect: "Did you help with the decorations?" *(Answer: Yes)*

Correct: "What were some of the items you and other students had to prepare for the Dinner and Dance?"

Be sure to go over the questions with your guests before recording them on camera. This solves two problems. One, it eliminates taking the time to record people on camera who have little or nothing to say. Two, it also eliminates the problem of the guest suddenly being "stumped" and not having an answer to one of the questions. Although the reporter may ask several questions of each guest, during the editing phase the interview will probably be narrowed down to one question.

Make sure you write down (and correctly spell!) everyone's name and title for later use in postproduction. It is very common to superimpose graphics over the images of guests as they are speaking on camera.

Reporter Tag

The closing or summary of your report needs to reflect the content of the rest of the project. The closing is a brief statement (two or three sentences) that the reporter makes on or off camera. It accomplishes two things. First, it summarizes the information in the report for the audience. Second, it provides the reporter a place to identify him- or herself and the station affiliation. This last part is known as the "tag." If you watch an ENG report on local or national news, the report will end with something similar to "This has been Ryan Charles reporting for NLPK News" or "For NLPK News, this has been Ryan Charles." Many reporters have gained notoriety for their creative tags on local and national news programs.

Producing the Story

Editing the parts of the report together is comparable to an artist creating a painting from a blank canvas or molding a beautiful vase from a lump of wet clay. The raw footage and story parts are edited together to create an informative and interesting news report.

Before the editing phase begins, the editor should preview (watch) all the raw footage and note the components that he or she will use to edit the finished report. Previewing the footage enables the editor to determine quickly which segments of the report will be used, saving time during the editing process. Only those components that are going to be used in the completed report will be accessed during the editing process. It is also helpful to develop a working storyboard or outline to follow during the postproduction.

Occasionally the reporter will work in conjunction with the editor during this phase. Editing "on the fly" (without an outline or storyboard) can be extremely difficult and actually make the editing process longer (Figure 5.11).

An ENG news report is like a story: it should have a beginning, a middle, and an end. The editor should carefully plan to edit the completed report so that it is informative and appealing to the audience. The pacing of the edited report is crucial to maintaining viewer interest. One technique often used in postproduction is referred to as The Rule of Threes. This rule states that the audio and video segments should be grouped in threes (sometimes this is even limited to twos), changing the format or style of the segments after every three sentences. For example, there would be three sentences of reporter standup, then

Fig. 5.11. A reporter and editor collaborate to produce ENG reports.

three sentences of reporter narration over footage, then two or three sentences of interviews or comments by guests, and finally three sentences of reporter standup summary. Following this rule keeps the report interesting by increasing the complexity and pace of the report and avoiding spending too much time (and script) on one component. The viewer's interest is maintained through the constant use of varying visual and auditory stimuli.

Let's look at an example of how the Rule of Threes would be followed producing an ENG report about the Annual International Dinner and Dance. Notice how each audio section uses two or three sentences to tell the story while changing the visual component as well.

1. *Lead-in* (reporter stand-up): "The foreign language teachers and students are arriving to enjoy the third annual International Dinner and Dance. This year's event is being held in the ballroom of the Grand Cyprus Hotel. An evening full of delicious international cuisine, dancing, and entertainment is planned."

2. *Comment 1* (student on camera): "We have worked for two months planning and preparing for tonight's big event, from the menus to the decorations."

   Comment 2 (teacher on camera): "Besides raising money for classroom activities and field trips, this event provides an excellent opportunity for students to experience and practice their foreign language skills."

   Comment 3 (parent on camera): "This dance gives parents and their children a wonderful learning experience that they can share together."

3. *Reporter Narration* (over video clips): "Ethnic foods on tonight's menu were kindly donated by restaurants in the city. But dining and dancing aren't the only activities to enjoy this evening! Foreign language skits, movies, and even a fashion show were included in this gala event."

4. *Closing* (reporter seated at table on camera): "The foreign language department would like to thank everyone who helped make this year's event a big success. As for me, I'm going to enjoy some of these culinary delights. For NLPK News, I'm [*reporter's name*]."

In this example, you can see how the completed edited report followed the Rule of Threes. As the viewer watches the report, both the audio and visual images will be changing from one format to another, creating interest and entertainment.

Another production technique involves the use of sound bites. As noted earlier, these are small segments (two to five seconds) of video and audio clips that remain intact and inserted in the project. In the report we just considered, sound bites can be inserted to convey the sights, sounds, and atmosphere of the evening. Small clips can be edited between some or all of the video and audio segments of the reporter and guests. Using sound bites enables viewers to experience the event as if they were there. Some good sound bites to use in this project might include the following:

- People dancing to ethnic music.

- Students performing a skit or modeling costumes in the fashion show.

- Some sights and sounds from the dining tables.

- Students engaging in foreign language conversations.

Carefully planning and producing an ENG project has a lot to do with how effective a report will be. Following the Rule of Threes can organize the information and presentation and eliminate a lot of the "what should we do next?" that comes with trying to edit a project without a guide or plan. Continuity results when the sequence and presentation of the material has been planned and produced professionally.

Postproduction Tips

1. Complexity is essential for maintaining viewer interest and attention. Edit camera angles and shots that portray the drama associated with the event. Avoid long camera pans and long, wide-angle shots that leave out detail. A series of two- to three-second shots is much more effective and informative.

2. Use graphics superimposed over video to identify the reporter, students, teachers, or other guests that appear on camera. A simple graphic that identifies the individual's name and title is effective. Graphics do not need to be left on the screen for the entire time the person is talking. They should be on long enough to read completely, say, three to five seconds. Examples:

   Ryan Charles

   NLPK Reporter

   Becky Beal

   Teacher

3. Use as much as the live sound as possible for background narration and sound bites. Inserting a "dubbed" track from a favorite CD usually changes the character and mood of the video.

4. Critically watch the completed video in its entirety. Don't be afraid to make changes to sections of the video that do not meet your expectations.

5. ENG reports are not documentaries, and their length should be approximately 60 to 90 seconds in total time. Avoiding longer segments and running times will help to keep your viewer interested.

Producing quality ENG reports enhances the effectiveness of school news shows and television production programs in general. Developing professional reporter and videographer skills and habits can prepare students for entrance to college or vocational programs and lead to careers in the television industry.

Review Questions

1. Define the following terms:

   ENG reporting

   Sound bite

   Stand-up

   Rule of Threes

   Talking head

2. Identify three ways you could research an upcoming report on the topic of "Teen Curfews."

3. Identify three tasks a reporter should complete during an ENG report.

4. Identify three tasks a videographer should complete during an ENG report.

5. Describe how an editor would utilize the Rule of Threes when producing an ENG report.

6. Describe three elements of recording and editing guests' comments and statements on camera to make them effective.

7. How are sound bites used effectively in creating ENG reports?

8. Write a sample reporter "lead-in" for the following topics. Remember to limit your lead-ins to two or three sentences.

   • Civic Club Car Wash (fundraiser)

   • SAT Preparation Class (Saturday mornings!)

   • Yearbook Delivery Day

   • Teacher of the Year

Student Project Plan: ENG Report with On-Camera Comments

Description of Completed Project

The student will produce a 60- to 90-second ENG report with the format and structure described in this chapter.

Format

Each report must contain the following:

1. Story lead-in (on-camera reporter stand-up): A two- to three-sentence lead-in describing the topic, event, or problem involved in the report.

2. On-camera comments, statements, or interviews: These are shot and edited clips of guests on camera discussing appropriate information about the topic. Shots may include interviews or "talking heads."

3. Reporter narration (off camera): A section of the report includes reporter narration over video clips of the activities being discussed. A variety of shots and camera angles should be used for inserted video clips.

4. Summary and Reporter Tag (on-camera): A two- to three-sentence summary of the event or topic, ending with the reporter's tag.

5. At least one sound bite must be included in the project.

Notes

1. Format should follow professional ENG reporting styles. Use of the Rule of Threes should be followed.

2. Total length of the report should not exceed 60 to 90 seconds.

Evaluation

The completed project will be worth 100 points.

- Reporting (25 points)
- Videography (25 points)
- Editing (25 points)
- Content (25 points)

Evaluation Sheet:
ENG Reporting with On-Camera Comments

Project Staff _____

Reporter/Writer _____

Videographer _____

Editor/Other _____

Reporting . . . . (25 points) _____

Is the research and information presented appropriate? Does the script follow a format? Is the reporter's on-camera appearance professional?

Videography . . . . (25 points) _____

Are shot composition, use of camera angles, and microphone sound consistently good? Are necessary activities and events videotaped?

Editing . . . . (25 points) _____

Does the report follow ENG format? Is the use of sound bites appropriate? Are editing continuity, use of graphics and titles, length successfully achieved?

Content . . . . (25 points) _____

Is the topic appropriate? Does the report have audience appeal? Is it informative? Is there appropriate use of comments and opinions?

Total Points Awarded . . . . (Out of 100) _____

Teacher Comments:

6 NONLINEAR EDITING

Objectives

After successfully completing this chapter, you will be able to

- list several reasons for editing in video production.
- describe a brief history of editing and explain how nonlinear editing differs from linear editing.
- describe the equipment used in nonlinear editing.
- explain the four-step method of nonlinear editing.
- list the options for recording the finished project and identify the best choice for specific production settings.
- list and explain several considerations for videography for an edited project.
- produce an edited instructional video program.

Vocabulary

clips bin. A section of the nonlinear editing system display screen that contains icons representing each audio, video, and graphic element available for use in the video project.

cut. One video shot appearing immediately after the previous video shot, with no apparent transition.

dissolve. A video transition in which the first video shot is gradually replaced by a second video shot, with no line of transition.

exporting. Recording a finished video program onto a medium such as videotape, DVD, or computer file.

IEEE-1394. A connecting device used to connect digital video camcorders to personal computers and nonlinear digital editing systems. The IEEE-1394 signal carries audio and video tracks and is capable of speeds up to 400 megabytes per second. Also known as "FireWire" and "iLink." (IEEE is the Institute of Electrical and Electronic Engineers, a technical/professional society.)

import, importing. The process of recording audio and video segments onto a hard drive (or other storage medium) for use in nonlinear digital video editing.

nonlinear digital video editing (also "nonlinear editing") . Postproduction work using audio and video elements saved as digital files on a computer hard drive or some other storage device. Nonlinear digital video editing is characterized by the ability to work on segments in any sequence (as opposed to traditional linear editing, which requires working from the beginning of the production until the end).

rendering. The process by which the nonlinear editing system (the computer) actually creates each transition, effect, or graphic.

trim. The editing technique of eliminating part of the beginning and/or end of a video or audio clip used in the nonlinear digital video editing process. "Trimming" a clip allows the editor to select exactly where the imported clip will begin and end.

wipe. A video transition in which the second shot gradually replaces the first shot on the screen, with a definite line of transition.

Many simple video projects can be completed with just a camcorder, tripod, and microphone, as described in previous chapters. Other projects, especially "live" programs such as news shows, debates, and sports events, can be produced with cameras, microphones, audio and video mixers, and character generators. Many of the complex programs that you will wish to produce require editing, however.

In this chapter, we'll look at the nonlinear editing process and how to use nonlinear editing in producing video segments. First, we'll look at the reasons that we chose to edit programs. Then we'll explain the process of nonlinear editing—from importing your audio and video sources, to exporting onto videotape or digital media. Finally, we'll walk through an edited video project to make sure you have a firm grasp on the nonlinear editing process.

Why Do We Edit?

Editing fulfills several functions in video production. Understanding why we edit—the goals we can achieve by editing—will help us when planning our video projects and allow us to make the best choices in the editing process.

Editing to Correct Mistakes

One of the most obvious reasons that we edit is to correct mistakes. Sometimes our reporter will make a mistake on camera, or our guest will lose his or her train of thought in the middle of an interview. Other mistakes include technical mistakes (camcorder or microphone problems), mechanical mistakes (a semitruck blowing its horn as you record your opening), and "mistakes of nature," such as a bird flying into the shot or a sudden thunderstorm.

Editing to Select the Best Take

When we shoot our video footage knowing that we will edit it later, we can shoot several "takes" (an event recorded on videotape) and select the best take during the editing process. For example, when recording your reporter's introduction, you might record a standard medium-shot stand-up. The second take may have the reporter walking as the videographer pans. A third take might be shot from a creative angle. During the editing process, each take can be examined, with the best take selected for use.

Editing to Add Detail

Editing allows us to add details to our projects—especially close-ups. During a video program called "How to Change a Tire," for example, the editor could include close-ups of the air-pressure gauge and the lug nuts.

Editing for Single-Camera Production

Even though the footage is shot from various angles, most small-scale video production is shot with a single camera. The videographer creates the first shot, pauses the tape, creates the second shot, pauses the tape, and so on until each shot is recorded on videotape. The alternative would be to set up two cameras and a video mixer—involving much more equipment and at least two more technicians. Editing allows us to seamlessly combine each segment shot with our single camera into a flowing program.

Editing to Shift Time

When we edit, we combine segments created over a long time period and make them appear as if they were shot continuously. Imagine you a creating a segment explaining the music classes in your school—concert band, jazz band, chorus, and electronic music. Each section begins with a brief introduction by your reporter, followed by shots of students in class and then a brief interview with the teacher. In our program, we want to create the feeling that we are going from room to room in the music wing to find out what's happening in each music room. The schedule just won't allow production in one day, however—the chorus has a performance on Wednesday; the jazz band visits the elementary school on Thursday—typical for a high school. Our video production crew can create the raw footage for the project over a period of several days. Editing allows us to shoot each segment when possible.

Editing to Create a New Program Using Old Resources

You've just finished a great "Welcome to Our High School" videotape for an audience of adults, to be shown at Parents' Night. Now your school guidance counselor wants to show the same program to incoming freshmen, but you're concerned that the some of the script details just aren't important to the ninth graders, and you'd like to change the music to reflect their styles and tastes. Editing will allow you to keep the appropriate elements and change only the parts you need to change.

Editing to Fit Time Requirements

Sometimes our video segments are just too long. Our assignment is to create a 45-second preview of the big game for the news show. We ask the coach a great open-ended question: "What's the plan for the big game tonight?" Much to our surprise, the coach goes on and on—and on! Our 45-second segment is now three minutes long. What can we do? Edit! Shoot a brief opening, shoot a brief conclusion, and pull out the best 15 seconds of the coach's comments. You can probably think of other scenarios when you'd need to edit for time reasons.

Editing to Add Graphics and Music

Most nonlinear editing systems, as described later in this chapter, allow you to add music and graphics to your programs.

Editing to Produce Creative, Effects-Filled Segments

Nonlinear editing systems also have a full palette of digital effects that allow you to change the color, speed, and overall look of your program. You can also insert transitions, such as wipes, spins, and dissolves, between each segment of your program.

Editing—How It Used to Be

Television broadcasts have been around for a long time. The technology to produce and broadcast television was developed in the 1920s and became widely available in the late 1930s. By the late 1940s, four networks—ABC, CBS, NBC, and DuMont—had regular broadcast schedules, including news, sporting events, game shows, comedies, and dramas. Many of these programs were produced live—the audience saw the program as it happened. More complex programs that required editing were shot on film. Editing film is a simple, somewhat primitive process. Film consists of individual pictures. Simply find the end of the sequence, and physically cut (with scissors or a knife) everything that follows. When you find your next segment, just glue it to the previous segment. Complex television programs were created this way for many years.

In the late 1960s, the use of magnetic videotape became common practice in television production. Now when we think of a videotape, we think of a videocassette with tape inside. Early videotape, however, was provided on open reels and had to be threaded through a videotape recorder. The tape itself was either two inches or one inch wide (compared with VHS videotape, which is ½ inch wide), and the videotape recorder was about the size of an average dining room table.

As we said earlier, film consists of individual pictures that you can see. In contrast, video technology records signals electronically on magnetic tape. You can't see the pictures on the tape. Also, the signals aren't recorded in a straight vertical pattern. Instead, they're recorded in a diagonal pattern called a helical scan. So even if you could see where to cut the videotape, you wouldn't be able to cut it correctly. To further complicate matters, the videotape contains a control track that synchronizes the picture with the TV. If that control track is cut, the picture will jump and swerve on the TV screen or monitor.

Until a few years ago, the only way to edit videotape was to make a copy. Two VCRs were connected together, and the desired segments were copied from the original videotape to the finished program using the VCRs' "play," "record," and "pause" buttons. Professional television stations and some schools used sophisticated VCRs connected to editing control units. An editing control unit is a small computer that controls where each VCR starts and stops. Using two of these advanced VCRs and an editing control unit, a video editor could create a fairly sophisticated program. Of course, this early system provided cuts-only editing (no fades, transitions, or wipes), no graphics, and only two audio tracks. The equipment in this system—the VCRs and editing control unit—was expensive. A basic system cost $15,000. Few schools could afford this equipment (Figure 6.1).

Fig. 6.1. The new and the old: nonlinear editing systems are much smaller than their linear predecessors.

Even with an advanced editing system in place, one of the biggest frustrations of editing was the linear nature of the process. By "linear," we mean "in a straight line." Each element had to be edited in the order that it would appear on the finished tape. The first scene had to be edited first, then the second scene, and so on. The editor had to plan each element of the program carefully before the editing process began. Of course, there's nothing wrong with planning—but imagine that during the editing process, your production team had a great new idea for the first part of the program. You would have two choices: abandon your creative inspiration or start from the beginning and reedit the entire project. Linear editing is like laying down train tracks. Segments must be added in the order that they will appear on the finished project. Each segment is electronically linked to the previous segment, and to the segment that follows it.

This linear drawback was especially frustrating in the school setting. The students would submit a finished project, and the instructor would have a few suggestions on how it could be improved. It was unlikely, however, that those improvements would ever be made. As you know, this would mean starting all over again, and most classrooms didn't have the time or equipment to make that happen. The students would just have to wait to use those suggestions on the next project.

As you probably know, much of the learning in video production comes from experimentation. "What would it look like if I started with this segment?" or "What would the viewer think if I inserted this segment in between these two?" With linear editing, you couldn't do that. The finished program was continuously created during the editing process. Students just had to live with their mistakes.

The expense and frustration of linear editing, coupled with the availability of fast, powerful inexpensive computers, paved the way for nonlinear editing. Nonlinear editing takes its name from what it's *not!* It is *not* linear editing. The editor has the ability to edit various segments at various times—adding each segment in the place that he chooses. We can work from the end of the project to the beginning. We can work from the middle to the ends. We can even work from the start to the finish.

With nonlinear editing, we can work in a sequence that fits the needs of the production team. We can also experiment with new techniques and shot sequences. More important, we can take our instructor's advice, and improve on our mistakes! Using nonlinear editing, the project isn't finished until it is recorded onto videotape. Even then, it can be rerecorded after changes have been made.

Nonlinear Editing Equipment

Now that we've learned the reasons for editing, and a little background on the nonlinear editing process, let's look at the equipment used in nonlinear editing.

All nonlinear editing requires a computer. All of the elements of your production—all visual images and sounds—are converted into computer files for use by the nonlinear editing software. There are really two options available to people who wish to buy a nonlinear editing system. The first is to buy a complete stand-alone system. This is a computer that has nonlinear editing as its only task (Figure 6.2). When you turn on this system, the nonlinear editing software loads, and the editing screen is displayed. The main advantage of the stand-alone system is that all elements in the system are designed to work together. There won't be any hardware communication problems or software conflicts. A stand-alone system rarely needs troubleshooting, and the manufacturers of these systems offer technical support on every feature in the system.

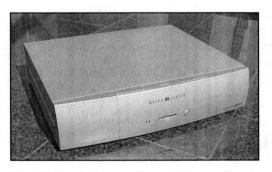

Fig. 6.2. Stand-alone nonlinear editing appliance.

The other option for nonlinear editors is to add editing software, and perhaps additional hardware, to your existing computer (Figure 6.3). Such additions might include an IEEE-1394 ("FireWire") interface, an advanced video card, an advanced sound card, and a large hard drive. In the past, building a computer to these standards was difficult. Most computers designed for home or school use were not built at the level required by nonlinear editing software. Now, however, many affordable computers are available that will edit video and run nonlinear editing software with little or no upgrading. All Apple computers currently on the market are designed to edit video, and most Windows-based computers are designed with video editing capabilities as well. Advanced computer operating systems, such as Windows XP and Mac OS X, have taken most of the struggle out of adding new hardware items to a computer, although sometimes hardware and software conflicts do occur. A big advantage of adding editing software to an existing computer is price. For less than $100, a school can convert a well-equipped desktop or laptop computer into an entry-level editing system. It is important to realize that editing software makes high demands on a computer system. Video editing will work better when all of the computer's RAM and processing power is available. Don't plan to surf the Web or create a PowerPoint presentation while editing video on your desktop computer.

Fig. 6.3. With minor upgrades, a desktop or laptop computer can be used as a nonlinear editing system.

There are other important items of equipment as well. A nonlinear editing system will require a VCR, and a computer monitor or video monitor (or both.) Your system might also require an audio mixer and external CD player if you wish to add voice and music.

The Nonlinear Editing Process

As described in the previous section, there are different options for nonlinear editing equipment. Some schools use stand-alone systems, such as Avio, Prestige, or Sequel. Other schools edit on Apple computers using iMovie, Final Cut Pro, or Premiere. Still other schools use Windows-based computers with a wide variety of editing software available. Therefore, a specific description of the editing process ("first click this button, then click that one") just isn't possible in a textbook designed for students using a variety of equipment and software. Nonetheless, the process of nonlinear editing is similar in each of the systems. In the next few paragraphs, we'll describe the nonlinear editing process to help you gain an understanding of how to create your video programs. It's up to your instructors to show you exactly which buttons to push on the system or software they've selected for your class.

The nonlinear editing process consists of four steps:

1. importing audio and video elements into a computer and saving them in a digital format;

2. arranging, deleting, and trimming audio and video elements;

3. adding transitions, effects, graphics, and sound; and

4. recording the finished program onto videotape or DVD, or saving it in a digital format.

Now, let's look at each step in a bit more detail.

Importing Audio and Video Elements and Saving Them in a Digital Format

As we said earlier, a nonlinear editing system is a computer. Therefore, every video and audio element you will use in your project must be converted into a computer file. These elements will probably include video footage from your camcorder, still images, music, and narration. Once the files are saved on you editing computer or system, you won't need the original videotape and music sources. The files are now saved on the computer's hard drive.

Different editing systems and computer programs save audio and video elements in different formats. Editing software might ask you how (which format) and where (on the hard drive) you want to save your elements. A stand-alone system simply saves the elements in a designated space on the system hard drive in a format designed for the system.

To import the audio and video elements, you will probably need to connect additional equipment to your editing system. Stand-alone systems typically have IEEE-1394 (FireWire), RCA composite, and S-VHS inputs for video, and RCA stereo inputs for audio (Figure 6.4). Some stand-alone systems have microphone jacks for direct importing of narration and built-in CD players for importing tracks from compact discs.

Fig. 6.4. Stand-alone nonlinear editing system inputs and outputs.

Input options on a desktop computer using editing software depend on the configuration of the computer (Figure 6.5). Most new computers have built-in IEEE-1394 (FireWire) cards. To input composite or S-VHS video, you might need to add a special video card to the computer. Music from a compact disc can be imported using the computer's CD-ROM drive. A microphone can probably be attached to the computer's sound card. Computers connected to a network can also import footage from a network drive. Editors working at multiple locations can all access the same video and audio elements. Although storing video and audio files on a network drive sound quite advanced to your school, realize that television networks, and even some schools, are already doing this. As hard drives become faster and cheaper, importing video and audio from a shared hard drive will become commonplace.

Importing audio and video elements is usually a simple task on a nonlinear editing system. First, the source for the element—a camcorder, a VCR, a microphone, and so on—is connected to the editing system. Then the user clicks an on-screen button, often labeled

Fig. 6.5. Inputs and outputs on a desktop computer designed for nonlinear editing.

"capture" or "record." The image or sound being imported can be seen or heard during the process. When the desired sequence has been imported, the user simply clicks the button again to stop the recording. An icon, or perhaps a small image, appears in an area of the monitor display called the "clips bin" for the user to access during the editing process. This process is repeated until all of the elements have been imported into the computer (Figure 6.6).

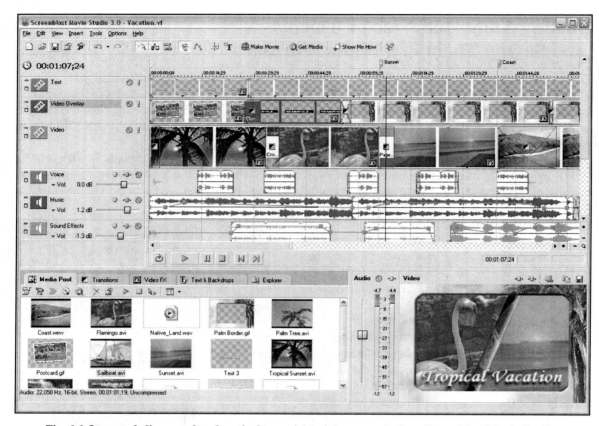

Fig. 6.6. Imported clips are placed on the lower right of the screen in Sony Screenblast Movie Studio.

Some nonlinear editing systems have automated the importing process when a digital video camera (for example, MiniDV) is used as a source, with an IEEE-1394 (FireWire) connector. Simply click the import button once, and the importing begins. A new clip is created in the clips bin every time the editing system detects a camcorder stop or start. So if you interview five of your fellow students and pause the tape after each interview during the videotaping process, those interviews will automatically appear as five separate clips in the clips bin when imported.

At this point, it's important to mention saving your work. Remember, a nonlinear editing system is a computer, and computer files need to be saved. Have you ever been working on a word-processing document or PowerPoint presentation, only to accidentally lose power or suffer a computer crash? Imagine how you'd feel if you lost all of the work you'd done on a video project! Some nonlinear editing systems—especially the stand-alones—automatically and continuously save your work. Some of the other systems do not. Make sure to find out this detail about your editing system, and get in the habit of saving your work every few minutes.

Arrange, Delete, and Trim Audio and Video Elements

Once all of the elements are in the "clips" bin, the editing process can begin. (You can continue to add additional elements throughout the editing process if you need to.) The icon representing each clip is inserted into a timeline on the screen using a "click, drag, and drop" process (Figure 6.7). Clips can be arranged in any order, previewed, and then rearranged if desired. It's a lot like building a jigsaw puzzle onscreen. Often there are separate audio and video sections of the timeline, so you can drag music files in the same space as video files.

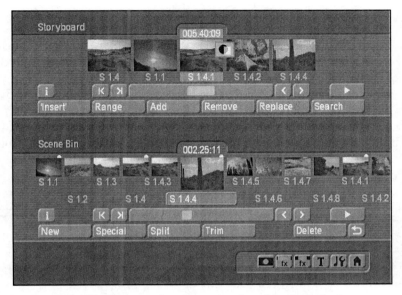

**Fig. 6.7. Clips are placed on a storyboard in the desired
order along the top of the Avio editing screen.**

Audio and video clips can be trimmed to make them shorter (Figure 6.8). Clips can also be split into two or more separate clips. Once you trim a clip, can you restore it to its original length? That depends on the nonlinear editing system you are using. Some systems replace the existing clip with the new, trimmed clip. This is called "destructive editing" because you are destroying the original clip. Of course, destructive editing saves hard drive space, and that's a major concern for some users. Find out if your editing system is destructive or nondestructive before making that first trim.

You probably won't use all of your clips. That's okay. Just leave them in the clips bin. You can delete them later. Some editors like to delete unwanted clips immediately, but you never know when you might need just a second or two of that footage. Better to leave them in the clips bin and delete them at the conclusion of the project.

After you complete this step, you should be able to watch your video program from start to finish. If you think about it, the program looks like it would if you had shot all the scenes in order, got everything right on the first take, and pressed the pause button at exactly the right time. Aren't you glad you have a nonlinear editing system?

**Fig. 6.8. Video clip trimmed in the
Avio editing system.**

Add Transitions, Effects, Graphics, and Sound

You've probably got a lot of effects and transitions available on your nonlinear editing system. You probably also have the ability to add graphics (words) and additional sound elements as well. Let's take a look at each of these and how they impact your program.

Transitions

A transition refers to the way we move from one video element to another. Transitions impact the emotions and intensity of your video project and should be selected with thought. In this section, we'll look at three types of transitions: cuts, dissolves, wipes.

Cut. A cut is really not a transition at all, but the absence of a transition. A cut is when one shot appears instantly after the previous shot (Figure 6.9). Cuts are used when no dramatic impact or emotion is desired. For example, if you are editing your school news show and you want to move from a shot of your first news reader to a shot of your second news reader, you would probably use a cut. Cuts are also used in sports, when there's plenty of action on the screen to keep the audience interested and fancy transitions would just get in the way.

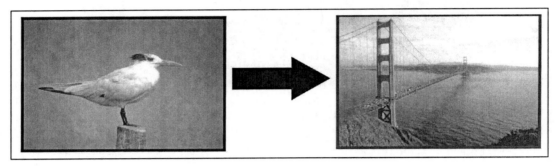

Fig. 6.9. Cut.

Cuts are also important because they take no time. Using cuts, you can show shots instantly. Imagine you want to make a really exciting opening sequence for a skateboarding video. You want to show 10 shots for a half second each. Could you dissolve between each of these shots? Probably not. The dissolve takes too much time and would undermine your objective: to create an exciting opening. A cut reflects real life and uses no time at all on your video project.

Dissolve. The most basic transition is the dissolve. With a dissolve, one video shot fades out as the second one fades in (Figure 6.10). On some nonlinear editing systems the speed of the dissolve can be adjusted, so that the dissolve happens very quickly, or very slowly.

Fig. 6.10. Dissolve.

A dissolve and a cut are often used in similar situations. As the names imply, the cut gives the viewer a much more abrupt feeling. Even the fastest dissolves give the sense of easing in to the next shot. A slow dissolve can have a dramatic effect on your video project. There's a bit of sadness when we see one scene slowly fade into another. A dissolve—either slow or fast—can also give the viewer a sense of change of time and place. Imagine a shot in which a young lady walks across the stage at her high school graduation. Let's say the script calls for the next shot to be set five years later, as the young woman sits in a downtown office. The dissolve helped the viewer make that mental transition.

As you probably already know, a dissolve can be made to a background color as well. This is called a "fade." If you want to fade to black, or fade from black, in your video, select the "black" clip (included in many editing systems), place it on the storyboard, and use the dissolve transition to accomplish the fade. If your editing system doesn't have a "black" clip, simply place the lens cap on your camcorder, click the "capture" button, and make one.

Wipe. A wipe is a transition in which the second shot gradually replaces the first shot on the screen, with a definite line of transition (Figure 6.11). The most common wipes are vertical and horizontal. Most nonlinear editing systems have several wipes available. Some of the wipes are simple—like a vertical or horizontal push. Others are quite complex, like page turns and spinouts.

Fig. 6.11. Wipe.

No matter which wipe you choose, remember this: the audience will be conscious of the wipe—more so than a dissolve or cut. Wipes definitely indicate a change in time and/or place. We expect to see a wipe between shots in different cities or shots that happened on different days. It would be very peculiar to see a wipe between close-ups of people sitting at the same table. Of course, you can use this video awareness to create a sense of heightened intensity and excitement in your action videos. A few well-placed wipes can certainly added to the thrill of your video program.

Effects

Effects change the appearance of your video segments. Some effects are designed to improve subtly the segment's color and brightness. Other effects, such as slow motion, fast motion, strobe, and blur change the way the viewer will perceive the motion on the screen. Other effects are much more obvious. Most nonlinear editing systems have a large palette of digital effects that can totally change the look of each video shot (Figure 6.12).

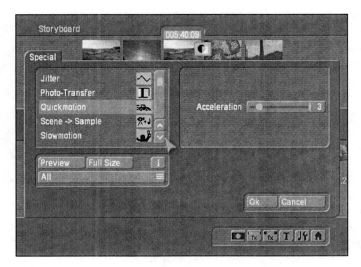

Fig. 6.12. Special effects can be added to individual video clips.

Some of the more advanced nonlinear editing systems are equipped with chroma key effect, in which the editor can replace any color in the shot (usually green) with another image. This is the famous weather map shot on the local news that features the weather forecaster walking in front of an animated weather map or graphic. Some systems also feature a moveable "blue box" into which a second image can be inserted. Of course, every system has a different assortment of effects.

With all of those effects at your fingertips, it's easy to get carried away and use too many of them. Make sure that when you add an effect, you're doing it for a reason. What are you trying to communicate with the effect? What do you want the audience to feel or think when they see it? It's fun to experiment with effects, but they can certainly distract the viewer from the original video. Use effects wisely.

Graphics

Most nonlinear editing systems have a graphics function that lets you type words on the screen. This is great for adding titles, credits, and captions (such as the name of the person on screen). When creating graphics, make sure to select colors that will create a high contrast with your background. Low-contrast graphics, such as pastel yellow letters on a light pink background, will be hard for your audience to read. Adding a border or drop shadow to your on-screen letters will help (Figure 6.13).

Fig. 6.13. Letter outlines can help increase text-to-background contrast.

Also, make sure your graphics are large enough to read at a distance. When you create the graphics, you will be only a few inches from the screen. Your audience will probably be seated several feet away. Create graphics that are easy for your audience to read.

A final note on graphics: if you plan to insert a graphic over a bust shot of a person (indicating the person's name, perhaps), you need to make sure you shoot the raw footage with that space left (Figure 6.14). This space for the graphic is called the "lower third," indicating that the lower one-third of the screen should be available for such a graphic. Plan your lower thirds before you shoot, and don't insert a graphic over someone's chin!

Fig. 6.14. Leave the lower third of the shot blank if you plan to add a graphic to a bust shot.

Rendering

Before we go on, we need to mention the concept of rendering. Rendering is the process by which the nonlinear editing system (the computer) actually creates the transition, effect, or title that you decide to use. Most nonlinear editing systems compress the audio and video elements to save hard drive space. When you select a transition between two shots (for example, a wipe), the computer decompresses the last few seconds of the first shot, decompresses the first few seconds of the second shot, rewrites those segments using the transition, and compresses the new file.

As you've probably guessed, these processes take time. Faster computer processors, larger RAM modules, and bigger hard drives make rendering much faster. Depending on your nonlinear editing system, it might take just a few seconds to render a simple transition. It might take several minutes to add an effect to a one-minute clip, however. (Many systems offer a quicker, low-quality preview of the transition, effect, or graphic before rendering.)

Rendering speed depends on the computer and the software. The best advice is to be selective in choosing your transitions, effects, and graphics. When you're short on time, don't add an effect "just to see what it looks like." Use your editing time wisely!

It's also important to point out that with some nonlinear editing systems, rendering is a destructive process. Imagine that you have decided to place a wipe in between two video segments. Then you decide you don't want the wipe; you'd rather leave it as a cut. With some systems, the part of each video clip used to create the wipe (maybe a half second of each clip) has been destroyed. That small amount of video might not be important, but it could also be very important. Make sure to determine whether your nonlinear editing system will restore the original clips after rendering—before you decide to render.

Sound

Your nonlinear editing system will probably allow you to add two or three tracks of sound to your program, in addition to the sound embedded on the original videotape. (Most nonlinear editing systems allow you to delete, or at least turn off, the sound from the videotape if you don't want to use it.) You might want to use these additional tracks to add music and sound effects.

Music and sound effects can be added in a variety of ways. If you are using a computer and software-based system, you will probably import music via the computer's CD-ROM drive or directly from music creation software (such as ACID®, Cakewalk, or Movie Maestro). Some stand-alone systems have built-in CD players, and others do not. If your system does not have a CD player, you can connect one to the audio inputs and capture music and sound effects that way. Other audio sources, such as audiocassette and MP3 players, can also be connected to the audio inputs of the nonlinear editing system. To add narration, locate the microphone jack on your nonlinear editing system (or on the computer's sound card). If a microphone jack is not provided, you can connect the microphone to a small audio mixer and connect the outputs of the audio mixer to the audio inputs of the nonlinear editing system.

Most nonlinear editing systems let you adjust the level of each audio track. You can play the music at full volume during the title graphic, then slowly fade out the music as the talent begins to speak.

If you plan to delete the sound entirely from a video track, make sure to delete that sound before you add a transition. As we stated earlier, the transition has properties of its own. The one-second transition will keep the audio, even if you've deleted it from the two clips.

Chose the music that you use in your video project carefully. Popular or famous songs might have meaning to your audience that has nothing to do with your video program. For that reason, we recommend using professional production music, as discussed in Chapter 3, for most of your video projects.

Record the Finished Program

You've done a lot of work on this project so far. You've imported your audio and video elements, you've trimmed the clips and assembled them in the order that you want. You added transitions, effects, graphics, and music. You've finished your project. The only problem—the project is still sitting on your nonlinear editing system. Unless your audience plans to peek over your shoulder or sit on your lap, you need to record the finished program onto a medium, such as videotape, DVD, or computer file.

Recording onto Videotape

The most common conclusion to a video project is to record the edited project onto videotape. If you have a camcorder or VCR that records in a digital format (such as MiniDV), this is easy. Just connect the IEEE-1394 (FireWire) cable to the nonlinear editing system and the recording device (camcorder or digital VCR) and click the appropriate on-screen button. This is the same connection that you used to import the video elements from your camcorder. The IEEE-1394 (FireWire) connector contains both the audio and video signals and is also input and output.

If you plan to record the project on a standard analog VCR, such as VHS and S-VHS, locate the correct outputs on the nonlinear editing system and connect them to the inputs on the VCR. You will probably have to press "record" manually on the VCR, then click the appropriate on-screen button.

What if you want to record your project onto VHS videotape (to share with family and friends at home), but you're using a computer/software-based nonlinear editing system that doesn't have video outputs? Simply record the program onto MiniDV videotape using the IEEE-1394 (FireWire) connector, then copy the program from MiniDV to VHS using a camcorder and VHS VCR.

If this is just a "practice" video project, you might want to record it to your VHS work tape. If this project is a "keeper," record it on the best format available. If your school uses MiniDV or S-VHS as a recording format, consider buying an extra videotape in one of those formats to archive your video projects. As you know, both MiniDV and S-VHS are much higher quality than VHS. Later, if you want to make a VHS copy, you will have the program recorded on a high-quality master videotape.

Creating a DVD

Many nonlinear editing systems, including stand-alone and software-based systems, are equipped with DVD burners. Blank DVD prices have dropped dramatically in recent years, and so have prices for DVD burners and players. If your school has decided to invest in this technology, consider recording your projects onto a DVD.

Exporting as a Computer File

As Internet connection speeds get faster and computer-delivered video gains popularity, exporting your finished project as a computer file becomes a desirable option. Many editing systems give you the ability to export your project as a file that can be played on a computer, burned onto a CD-ROM, e-mailed, or uploaded to a Web site. Popular file formats include QuickTime (*.mov), RealMedia (*.rm), and Windows Media Video (*.wmv). You've probably downloaded video files from the Internet, and you know what kind of quality you usually get—not very good. Of course, we're not suggesting that you export your project as a computer file instead of recording to a videotape or DVD. Think of it as a bonus.

The big issue with computer video is file size. Even a small video file takes a lot of computer memory. It also requires a considerable amount of time to compress the video into a computer file. The two main issues in exporting a video to computer file are image size and frame rate.

Image Size. At what size is your computer monitor set? Probably something like 1024 x 768. Most videos saved as computer files are much smaller. The largest size you're likely to encounter is 720 x 480. Other sizes include 320 x 240 (CD-ROM movie), 240 x 180 (Web movie), and 160 x 120 (e-mail movie) (Figure 6.15). As we'll see later, the image size greatly influences the file size.

Fig. 6.15. Computer image sizes
include: 720 x 480, 320 x 240,
240 x 180, and 160 x 120.

Frame Rate. NTSC video (as seen in the United States, Japan, and several other countries) is recorded at 30 frames per second. When saving a video program as a digital file, a slower frame rate, such as 15 frames per second, is selected. Fifteen frames per second is noticeably "jerky" but still watchable (and Internet audiences have come to accept this level). Frame rates of 12 and 10 frames per second can be used, but the loss in quality is quite noticeable.

Image size and frame rate work together to effect file size. The following chart illustrates the file size for a one-minute video segment saved in the QuickTime format.*

	Image Size	**Frame Rate**	**File Size (One-Minute Video)**
E-mail movie	160 x 120	10	790 KB
Web movie	240 x 180	12	1.3 MB
CD-ROM movie	320 x 240	15	4.5 MB
Full quality	720 x 480	30 (29.97)	260 MB

So your four-minute video project will take about 18 MBs of space if saved in the CD-ROM Movie mode. (A blank CD-ROM has about 650 MB of usable space.) Your four-minute video would not fit on the CD-ROM if saved in the full-quality mode.

Let's look at another application. Let's say you save your four-minute video project as a QuickTime movie on the Web Movie setting. That will take a little over 5 MB of memory, which could easily be uploaded to your school or personal Web site. Sure, the image would be small, and the image quality wouldn't be that great. But now anyone on the planet with an Internet connection could download and watch your video project.

Also, portable memory storage devices are getting more powerful and less expensive (Figure 6.16). At the time of this writing, a 256-MB USB storage device sells for less than $50, and a 40-gigabyte external hard drive about the size of a 3 x 5 note card sells for around $100. Those prices will probably continue to drop. In theory, you could save all of your video projects in QuickTime format on one of these storage devices.

The only downfall to exporting in a digital format is the compression time. It may take several minutes for your computer to compress your video file and save it in one of the formats mentioned in this section. As computer speed gets faster, however, we can expect those times to decrease.

Exporting your finished project to a digital file format (such as QuickTime, RealMedia, or Windows Media Video) is a great way to share your files over distances and provides another way to show off your work.

After Recording

If you're using your school's nonlinear editing system, you'll probably need to delete your files after you record your project. This is an unfortunate reality of nonlinear editing in the school setting. Because hard drive space is limited and several students will need to share a nonlinear editing system, many projects are simply erased. Of course, the portable hard drives just described would be a great way for you to save your files.

Fig. 6.16. Portable storage devices: a USB pen drive and a USB/FireWire external hard drive.

*From Pogue, David. *iMovie2: The Missing Manual.* Sebastopol, CA: Pogue Press/O'Reilly, 2001.

Walk Through a Project

Now that we've explained the nonlinear editing process, let's briefly walk through a video project that you might be asked to make for your school. You have been assigned the task of creating a 5-minute video about your school's volleyball team. The team had a very successful season and won the district championship. Your project will include highlights from training camp, the regular season, and the district tournament, as well as brief interviews with the coach and team captain. Your program will include a title screen, lower-third graphics, and music. All of the video has been recorded, including footage provided by parents, the team videographer, and the two interviews that you recorded yourself.

Your first step is to import all of the elements into your nonlinear editing system. Let's imagine you're using a stand-alone system with a complete array of inputs. The videotape from training camp was recorded by a parent on VHS-C videotape. You borrow the VHS-C camcorder from the parent and connect the audio and video outputs to the inputs on the nonlinear editing system. The regular-season and tournament footage shot by the team videographer is on SVHS. You can connect an SVHS VCR to the SVHS inputs on the nonlinear editing system and capture that footage. Finally, you import your interviews shot on MiniDV via the nonlinear editing system's IEEE-1394 (FireWire) connector. Now, all of your video has been captured by the nonlinear editing system.

Because you connected both the audio and the video cables when you imported your video elements, much of the audio has already been imported as well. You can add music to your program in a variety of ways, as described earlier in this chapter.

With all of your audio and video elements imported into the nonlinear editing system and saved as digital files, you can begin the task of trimming and arranging the shots you want to use and deleting the scenes you don't want. Transitions are added between several of the action shots and effects are added to some of the shots as well. The color is a bit out of balance on some of the shots, and you use the nonlinear editing system's color correction function to bring them into balance.

Now it's time to add the graphics. You're keeping it pretty simple on this one—a title screen at the beginning and a simple "produced by" credit at the end (making sure to credit everyone who provided video footage, of course) and lower-third graphics superimposed over the interviews of the coach and the team captain.

You've decided to use a couple of music pieces—one you selected from your school's production music collection, and another that you made using Movie Maestro software. You make sure to lower the volume on the music track when the coach and team captain speak during their interviews.

After watching the video several times, asking your instructor for feedback, and making a few changes, you pronounce the program finished. You connect the MiniDV camcorder to the nonlinear editing system and record the finished program on MiniDV videotape. This way, you have a high-quality master tape from which you can make VHS copies later. You also decide to burn a DVD to play at the volleyball awards banquet. Finally, you export the video as a QuickTime movie, using the "Web movie" setting (240 x 180, 12 frames per second). Your five-minute highlight video takes about 6.5 MB of memory. The file is uploaded to your school's Web site for sharing with friends and family across the country.

Shooting Tips for Nonlinear Editing

This seems like an odd section to put at the end of the chapter, doesn't it? Of course, you want to shoot great video before you begin the nonlinear editing process. Your instructor probably asked you to read this chapter before you begin your next video project, so we thought we'd put our shooting tips here, so they'd be fresh on your mind as you begin creating your project.

Tip 1. Shoot various angles of the same action. This will give you several "looks" in your clips bin when it comes time to edit. As the videographer, you will need to ask your talent to "stop" and "do that over again" after you reposition your camera angle.

Tip 2. Planning is important. In an earlier chapter, we talked about storyboarding. Storyboarding is important in the shooting process, even if you plan to edit. Make sure you get all of the shots you need during your shooting session.

Tip 3. Be aware of continuity. Make sure clothing, props, and body positions are consistent throughout the program, even if you shoot on different days. For example: the video footage for "How to Change a Tire" might be shot over several days. Make sure that your tire changer (talent) wears the same clothes each day. If your talent is holding the tire iron in her left hand on the first shot, make sure the tire iron is still in her left hand in the second shot. You get the idea. Your audience expects the project to be consistent throughout.

Tip 4. Plan to show detail. Using a nonlinear editing system gives you a great opportunity to show your audiences close-ups of the action. Make sure to shoot those close-ups during production.

Tip 5. Shoot the creative shot. Because you're editing, you don't have to use every shot. This might be a good time to get creative with some aspects of videography. If it doesn't work, just delete it. Of course, keep in mind that safety is always important! Never do something dangerous just to get a great shot.

Tip 6. Roll plenty of videotape. When you're shooting video for a project that you plan to edit, make sure to roll tape about five seconds before the action begins and about five seconds after the action has concluded. This compensates for your camcorder's startup and rollback time, and makes sure you get the scene that you want.

Tip 7. Remember your lower third. If you're videotaping a person and you plan to superimpose a graphic below his or her face, make sure to leave the lower third of your shot empty for this purpose. Of course, this has to be done while you shoot. The easiest solution is to use a bust shot instead of a close-up (see Chapter 1).

Tip 8. Use good videography techniques, even if you're editing. You might think that you can slack off on your videography since you're editing the project, but that's simply not true. You should always use your best videography skills. Try to make every shot count. Some videographers will just say, "We'll fix it when we edit." This leads to a very frustrating editing session, as you try to sift through a tape full of bad shots to find two or three useable segments. Make the editing process a fun and creative time by giving yourself a number of shots with which to work.

Nonlinear editing systems are powerful tools for video professionals and students. Apply all of the skills that you've learned so far in this book, and your edited projects will be outstanding.

Selected Manufacturer Web Sites

Apple Final Cut Express http://www.apple.com/finalcutexpress
Apple Final Cut Pro http://www.apple.com/finalcutpro
Apple I-Movie http://www.apple.com/imovie
Applied Magic (Screenplay and Sequel) http://www.applied-magic.com
MacroSystem (AVIO and Prestige) http://www.casablanca.tv
Pinnacle Systems http://www.pinnaclesys.com
Roxio http://www.roxio.com
Screenblast® Movie Maker http://www.screenblast.com

Review Questions

1. List the eight reasons for editing provided in the text. Write them in the order that you think they contribute to the editing process. In other words, which one is most important? List them in that order.

2. "Nonlinear editing" is editing using a computer, software, and computer files. What is the importance of the word "nonlinear?"

3. What are two types of nonlinear editing systems? Which type does your school use?

4. Name three video inputs that should be present on all nonlinear editing systems.

5. List two other common names for importing video and audio into the nonlinear editing system.

6. Why is trimming an important part of the nonlinear editing process?

7. Name the three categories of transitions discussed in the text.

8. How is a dissolve different from a wipe?

9. What two questions should you ask yourself before adding a digital effect to a clip?

10. What three computer components affect rendering speed?

11. Why must we be careful when using popular or famous songs in our video productions?

12. What three options are explained in the text for recording your finished project?

13. What is the easiest way to record a finished project onto MiniDV videotape?

14. Name three popular file formats mentioned in the text for exporting your finished project as a computer file.

15. What are the two factors that determine file size when exporting a video project as a computer file?

16. Name the two storage devices mentioned in the text for archiving your video projects.

17. Imagine that you are making a video project about the animals in the local zoo. The host travels throughout the zoo talking about the various animals on display. Shooting is scheduled to take place over several days. Name three continuity issues that must be considered for this project.

18. Why does editing give the videographer the freedom to experiment with different techniques and camera angles?

19. One of the shooting tips for nonlinear editing is "Remember your lower third." Explain this in your own words.

Student Project Plan

Instructional Video

Description of Completed Project

The finished project will be a 3- to 5-minute edited video program instructing the audience on a certain task. The project must include at least five cameras angles. The project must also include a title screen, music, narration, at least one screen of internal graphics, and ending credits.

Method

1. A group of two students will select a topic for the instructional video. Select a concrete task—something that people actually do—rather than an abstract task. For example, "How to Make a Paper Airplane" is a concrete task. "How to Be a Good Friend" is an abstract task.

   Topic selection is *very* important for this video project. The audience should be able to at least attempt to do the task after watching your video program.

2. Storyboard the project. Select the best location. Make a list of all the materials you will need. You might also need to plan for several takes, so that you can repeat your task using several camera angles.

3. Shoot the videotape for this project.

4. Edit the program on your nonlinear editing system, using the four-step method describe in this chapter.

5. Submit the finished program for grading. Make sure to turn in your storyboards.

Evaluation

The completed project will be worth 200 points. Each team member will receive the same grade.

- Instructional value (50 points)
- Graphics (25 points)
- Audio (25 points)
- Editing (25 points)
- Videography (25 points)
- Script (25 points)
- Storyboards (25 points)

Evaluation Sheet: Instructional Video

Names _____ Date _____

Instructional Value . . . . **(50 points)** _____
   Appropriate task. . . . .(10 points) _____
   Step-by-step process . . . .(10 points) _____
   Appropriate rate. . . . .(10 points) _____
   Did we learn?. . . . .(20 points) _____

Videography . . . .**(25 points)** _____
   Shot selection. . . . .(10 points) _____
   At least five angles. . . . .(5 points) _____
   Focus . . . .(5 points) _____
   Appropriate detail . . . .(5 points) _____

Script. . . . .**(25 Points)** _____
   Appropriate amount. . . . .(10 points) _____
   Good explanation. . . . .(10 points) _____
   Appropriate style . . . .(5 points) _____

Audio. . . . .**(25 Points)** _____
   Mixing levels . . . .(10 points) _____
   Narration performance. . . . .(5 points) _____
   Music selection . . . .(5 points) _____
   Overall polish. . . . .(5 points) _____

Graphics . . . .**(25 points)** _____
   Title screen. . . . .(5 points) _____
   Internal graphics. . . . .(10 points) _____
   Credits . . . .(10 points) _____

Editing. . . . .**(25 points)** _____
   Technical quality . . . .(10 points) _____
   Program length. . . . .(10 points) _____
   Pace . . . .(5 points) _____

Storyboards. . . . .**(25 points)** _____
   Completion. . . . .(15 points) _____
   Visual. . . . .(5 points) _____
   Audio . . . .(5 points) _____

Total Points Awarded . . . . **(Out of 200)** _____

7 STUDIO PRODUCTION

Objectives

After successfully completing this lesson, you will be able to

- identify video mixer components, functions, and operations.
- identify and define lighting elements and fixtures.
- identify and describe studio personnel and tasks.
- understand and execute basic studio camera movements.
- successfully complete a studio production.

Vocabulary

backlight. A light used in production that is positioned behind the talent and designed to eliminate the shadows caused by the key light on background sets and curtains.

bank. A pair of buses, as on a video mixer.

blocking. Planning movements and actions of talent and crew.

bus. A row of buttons located on a video mixer that select video inputs.

cut. A video transition in which one video source instantly and completely replaces another.

cyclorama (Cyc). Large, seamless cloth or curtains that are hung on tracks to provide backgrounds for studio sets.

dissolve. A video transition in which one video source fades out as another fades in.

fade. A video transition in which one video source is gradually replaced on the screen by a background color, most often black. A fade is a dissolve to a background color.

fader bars. Levers located on a video mixer that activate buses and can be used to perform mixer operations and effects.

fill light. A third light used in studio production designed to fill in and eliminate shadow areas caused by the use of a key light.

flats. Wooden frames containing fabric or other lightweight materials used as backgrounds for studio sets.

121

gels. Colored squares of plastic material used on the front of lights to provide colored lighting on backgrounds and sets.

key. A function on a video mixer that enables graphics or other video elements to be superimposed on video or colored backgrounds.

key light. The main source of illumination in a video production, usually facing the on-camera talent.

line-out. A video mixer bus that directs the video source to the recording or broadcasting unit.

pan. A side-to-side camera movement as the camera base remains stationary.

preview bus. A video mixer bus that enables the previewing of camera angles, videotaped segments, graphics, or effects prior to being accessed to the line-out.

scrim. A fiber or plastic covering placed on the front of a lighting fixture to diffuse or "spread out" the light.

slate. A small blackboard-like device recorded on camera that gives program information (name, title, date, take numbers).

spotmeter. A device that measures the intensity of reflected light, as on a lighted set.

teleprompter. An electronic version of cue cards; the talents' script is displayed and manipulated on a computer monitor or refracted through a glass or mirror in front of the camera lens.

tripod dolly. A tripod mounted on a dolly base (spreader) that allows easy rolling of the camera from one position to another on the studio floor.

truck. A lateral movement of the camera achieved by moving or rolling the tripod dolly to the left ("truck left") or right ("truck right") .

wipe. A video transition in which one video source is replaced by another with a definite line of transition. Wipes often occur as a pattern or shape of a transition.

Producing television programs is an exciting and challenging responsibility. Studio production involves a lot of creative and technical expertise, as well as social and management skills in working with talent and production personnel. Successful studio production requires the coordinated effort from a variety of on-camera and production personnel. Each team member must successfully perform and coordinate his or her tasks from program conception to program completion.

Studio Production Equipment

Throughout this textbook, you have been introduced to a variety of video production equipment: camcorders, microphones, audio mixers, and character generators. The skills and expertise needed to operate each of these components is essential to successful production of a studio program. Each of these components is integrated into a studio production system and utilized during program production. There are, however, a few components used in studio production that have not been discussed in previous chapters. These include video mixers, studio lighting fixtures, sets and backdrops, and teleprompting devices.

The Video Mixer

Video mixers enable the production crew to select and use multiple video sources at the same time to tape and record an event or program. These sources can be combined to produce a variety of transitions and special effects, as well as changes in camera angles and positions during production. The number of video sources that a video mixer can use varies with the model and complexity of the device (Figure 7.1). Video mixers that contain several (three or more) video inputs allow more flexibility and greater complexity in designing and producing your programs. Video sources include cameras (both digital and video), VCR/DVD players, character generators, and even computers. All video mixers are designed to help the producer perform several basic functions, including the following:

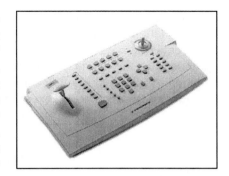

Fig. 7.1. Videonics MX-Pro digital video mixer.

- Select appropriate video sources from a variety of choices

- Perform video transitions from one source to another

- Create special effects

Using a video mixer during production enables the producer to utilize several video cameras and camera angles without editing, access graphics during production, and incorporate a variety of video sources without postproduction. Not only does this greatly reduce the time of production, but it can also reduce the costs associated with real-world postproduction. Many of the video mixers available today also offer an assortment of special effects that can be simultaneously accessed during production.

Although video mixers vary in their design and features, most functions are comparable from model to model. Each video input (camera, character generator, VCR) is delegated to a button located on one of the mixer's buses (a row of buttons on a video mixer). Pressing that button accesses that particular video input. Some video mixers may contain several rows of buses. In this case, a fader bar is used to select or activate the desired bus. By moving the fader bar up or down, the selected buses are activated. Sometimes two or more buses, or rows of buttons, are used at the same time to create an effect. In this case, they are referred to as a bank. Video mixer banks are used for effects like chroma keys and superimpositions.

Video mixers also contain a preview bus. This bus routes the video signal to a preview monitor that enables the technical director to "see" or preview a source (camera angle, graphic, videotape) or effect before accessing it. This is especially helpful in ascertaining whether the forthcoming video segment is properly cued and ready, if the graphics are prepared for keying, or if the next camera shot and angle are appropriately framed. Many video mixers now digitally create a "preview screen" that includes all the video inputs and a multitude of effects. This eliminates the need for a "preview" monitor for each source and enhances the technical director's control over the mixer's functions and effects.

The program bus, or line-out, directs the selected video source to the recording or broadcast device. A line-out monitor is essential for scrutinizing the video and audio signals of the completed program as it is being recorded or broadcast. Video mixers may also have the line-out options listed as program, main out, or both (Figure 7.2).

Fig. 7.2. The technical director observes the preview and line-out monitors during production.

Video Mixer Operation

Certain standard video mixer operations can be performed on most video mixers available in television production programs. These would include cuts, dissolves, fades, and wipes.

A cut is an instantaneous switch from one video source to another. Cuts are used for a rapid change in camera angles, as in a talk or variety show. The video simply "cuts" from one shot to another, with no transition. A cut is achieved by simply pressing another video source button (a camera, for example) on the same bus or row that is currently activated (Figure 7.3).

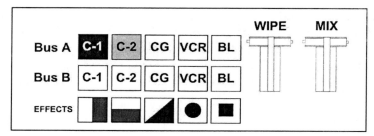

Fig. 7.3. Video mixer operation for a cut.

For example, Camera 1 is activated in Bus A. To cut to Camera 2, the technical director would simply press the Camera 2 button in Bus A. The program monitor will now show camera 2 instead of camera 1. The fader bar is not used to produce a cut.

A dissolve is a transition from one video source to another where the images will overlap at some point. To perform a dissolve, a video source is activated on Bus A and the second source to be dissolved into is selected on Bus B. The fader bar (mix function) is then moved from Bus A to Bus B, thereby dissolving the sources from one to another (Figure 7.4).

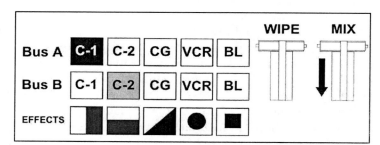

Fig. 7.4. Video mixer operation for a dissolve.

The slower the fader bar is moved, the slower the dissolve. Some mixers contain an adjustable automatic speed control for setting the speed of dissolves, wipes, and fades. If you stop a dissolve at midpoint between the two images, you have created a "super." A super allows you to see both images occurring simultaneously, one on top of the other.

A fade is accomplished in much the same way as a dissolve, but instead of dissolving to another video source, the fade is dissolved into a solid background color, usually black. Most video mixers contain a button or source for obtaining black or background color. If none are available, a blank black screen composed on a character generator will work (Figure 7.5).

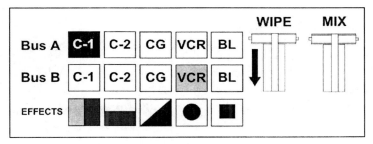

Fig. 7.5. Video mixer operation for a fade.

For example, Camera 1 in Bus A is currently activated. By pressing the button in Bus B labeled "BL" for black and moving the fader bar (mix) down, the Camera 1 shot will fade to black.

Video mixers designate dissolves, fades, and supers as "mix" functions. Look for a separate fader bar labeled "mix" or a button that delegates the mix function to the mixer's fader bar if there is only one fader bar on the mixer.

Wipe functions generally include wipes, keys, and some special effects. During a wipe, one video picture seems to push another off the screen. Wipes can be achieved in a variety of patterns and shapes depending on the complexity of the video mixer being used for the transitions (Figure 7.6). For example, to "wipe" from Camera 1 to a video segment, the following steps would be performed:

1. Select the VCR button on Bus B.

2. Select a wipe pattern to be used from available effects on the mixer.

3. Move the fader bar (wipe function) from Bus A to Bus B.

Fig. 7.6. Video mixer operation for a wipe.

Another video mixer operation that is often used during productions is "keying," which refers to the process of electronically cutting out portions of a video picture and filling them in with graphics or other video images. Typical video mixer key effects used in productions include the following:

- **Wipe Key:** allows the keying of graphics and video to occur while using one of the wipe patterns available on the video mixer.

- **Matte Key:** allows the cutout portions of the video image to be "filled in" with a selected color generated by the video mixer.

- **Chroma Key:** allows the use of a color background (hence the word *chroma*, the Greek word for "color") to be used to create the key effect. This is commonly called "blue screen." For example, an actor stands in front of a colored background (usually blue or green) on camera. A selected background image supplied by a VCR or computer can be "keyed" in, thereby replacing the colored background with the new image. A good daily example of this effect is your local weather forecast. The weather reporter is actually standing in front of a colored background and the weather maps and graphics are keyed in electronically to produce the picture you see at home. The actor actually looks at a television monitor off to the side to orient his or her actions on the screen.

Video Mixers and Digital Video Effects

Video mixers are frequently called on to create special effects during production. The advent of chip technology and DVEs (digital video effects) has created the ability to turn normal (analog) video signals into a digital (numerical) signal. By digitizing the video information, the mixer can manipulate the signal, store the signal, then retrieve the signal on command. Some of the following special effects are routinely used in television production:

- **PIP (picture in a picture):** the DVE can place and resize another image to fit anywhere on the screen over the existing image. Common examples include those graphics you see "placed" over the anchor's shoulders on local and national newscasts.

- **Posterization:** sometimes referred to as "paint," the DVE manipulates the brightness and shading of the picture area to create a painted, posterlike image.

- **Mosaic:** the DVE divides the picture into minute squares, or tiles, to obtain a mosaic tile look.

- **Strobe:** sometimes referred to as "stop-action," the video appears to jump from one video frame to another. The amount of time (video frames) between frames elapsed during playback can be increased or decreased with an adjustment on the video mixer.

The advent of digital video has led to the development and use of sophisticated software-based video mixers. The video mixer is actually a computer-based model of the hardware described in this chapter. Rather than pushing and pressing buttons and fader bars, you can use a mouse to access video sources and effects (Figure 7.7). Software-based systems can be easily and regularly upgraded when new software is written rather than purchasing an upgraded version with hardware-based equipment. With most software-based systems, it's also possible to go beyond basic mixing and create such effects as three-dimensional illustrations and animation.

Fig. 7.7. Software-based video mixer.

Technical Direction and Communication

During the course of a program, dozens (if not hundreds) of mixes and effects from one video source to another may occur. It is the role of the director to orchestrate the technical crew in the operations of production. Communication is essential between technical crew and talent for television production. The producer/director (usually the same student will fill both of these roles) needs to be able give directions and coordinate production activities during the taping. There are two basic types of systems available for production: wired and wireless intercom systems. Wired systems, commonly referred to as a PL (private line or production line) systems, can be found built-in on most broadcast quality video mixers and cameras (Figure 7.8). These headset and microphone systems will plug into a jack designed to accommodate them on the video mixer and studio cameras. The director can speak with and communicate cues to the technical director and camera operators, as well as the floor director. If the video mixer and cameras being used in the studio are not fitted with a built in "talk-back" system, a separate wired system can be purchased that operates independently from the video equipment. One benefit of such a system is that it can be moved and used at another location (gym, theater, football field) when needed. The crew's communications are transmitted via cables and headsets. The wired systems components will include the following:

- **Main Station:** The main station controls and supports the individual headsets and allows the crew members to communicate with one another. Each individual's headset (earphone and microphone) is connected to the station. All crew members connected to the system can communicate with each other. The main station usually requires AC or DC power sources and provides power to the individual headsets; it is usually situated in the production control room.

- **Belt Packs:** The belt pack is connected to the main station via a microphone cable. Cable length determines how far each crew member can travel from the main station. Directors and technical crew members need shorter cable than the camera operators, who are located in the studio and require more freedom of movement.

- **Headsets:** Each crew member's headset is complete with an ear piece to hear commands and instructions and a microphone to speak to other crew members. The headset is attached to the belt pack. Most headsets can be activated with a voice or manual control. More expensive models allow you greater control over volume (speaking and listening) and are generally more comfortable and durable.

Fig. 7.8. A wired intercom system is often used for studio production.

Fig. 7.9. A wireless intercom system.

Wireless intercom systems use radio frequencies that actually broadcast the signals from one unit to another (Figure 7.9). It is important to purchase all your headsets with the same channel frequency. The range and quality of these systems vary greatly across manufacturer and price. They are very practical in situations when using wired intercom cable is difficult (e.g., stadiums, gymnasiums, across water). Although generally less expensive than wired intercom systems, wireless intercom systems have some distinct disadvantages:

- They are susceptible to interference from other communication devices, as well as electronic interference from lighting and sound systems.

- They may not be able to transmit well between walls and glass.

- Each headset requires its own power source (generally a 9-volt battery). Once the battery weakens, the headset's range and efficiency is diminished.

- They tend to be less sturdy and durable than most wired intercom headsets.

The director's instructions must be succinct and clearly phrased, giving all crewmembers the time and direction they need to perform their duties. This is especially true for the technical director, the person operating the video mixer. The technical director must be told what video source is to be accessed, when it is to be accessed, and how the transition is to occur each and every time a transition is needed (Figure 7.10). Cues such as "ready," "standby," and "take" are often used between director and technical crews during the course of a production. Here is a brief look at how a director would use cues to produce a talk show:

Director's Cues	Application
"Standby in the studio"	Everyone on crew remains quiet and attentive, ready for production to begin in 15 to 30 seconds.
"Recording black"	Videotape operator starts recording. Technical director has black accessed on video mixer.
"Ready to roll tape opening"	Videotape operator prepares to play tape for show opening. Technical director prepares to access VCR on video mixer.
"Roll show opening ... dissolve "	Videotape operator plays show opening. Technical director dissolves from black to show opening.
"Ready Camera 1"	Camera 1 has shot and angle framed and ready. Technical director prepares to transition to Camera 1 on director's cue.
"Dissolve 1"	Technical director dissolves from show opening to Camera 1 (close-up of host).
"Ready to go 2"	Camera 2 has shot framed (two shot of host and guest). Technical director prepares to go to Camera 2 (cut) on director's cue.
"Go 2"	Technical director "cuts" to Camera 2.

During the course of the production, the director is always thinking ahead and then cueing the crew to the necessary steps to achieve the transition. It is important for the director to remain calm and poised and to communicate constantly with the technical crew so that everyone is aware of what happens next on the production agenda.

Fig. 7.10. The director communicates instructions to studio personnel.

Teleprompter

Actors and on-camera talent usually rely on several methods for writing and reading their script: cue cards, teleprompters, note cards, and pure memorization. Of these methods, the most common and reliable method is the teleprompter. Today's teleprompters rely on some computer-driven text system that is displayed in front of the camera lens via a glass/mirror system. The video image from a computer monitor is reflected onto a glass/mirrored surface mounted at a 45-degree angle in front of the camera lens. The teleprompting software allows the text to be displayed in reverse-image (backwards), so that when it is reflected on the glass, it appears right-side up. The camera literally "shoots" through the glass, so the talent can appear to be looking directly into the camera lens while actually reading the script (Figure 7.11). A teleprompter operator manipulates the script, controlling the speed and starting and stopping the script as videotaped segments are played. Each studio camera should have its own teleprompter monitor; the teleprompter operator and the technical crew also need a monitor to follow as the show progresses. The advent of electronic text software has made it easy to fine-tune scripts and make last-minute changes, compared with older models that actually used a hard-copy (printed) script that was videoed by an actual camera and displayed on a monitor. The software also contains features that provide for more than one on-camera speaker, such as underlining, highlighting, or colorizing (Figure 7.12). For example:

SPEAKER 1: Hello, and welcome to [plain text]. Good Morning NorthLake.

SPEAKER 2: **We hope you enjoyed [highlighted text] your holiday weekend!**

When using a teleprompter, position the camera close enough to the talent for them to be able to read the text without the viewer being able to detect the left-to-right movement of their eyes as they read. Generally, the camera is placed a slight distance from the talent, and the camera is "zoomed in" slightly to provide a close-up shot of the talent.

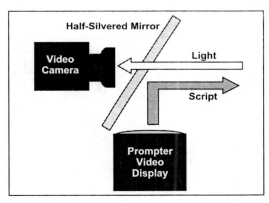

Fig. 7.11. Teleprompting system diagram.

Fig. 7.12. Sample teleprompting screen.

Lighting

Although most camcorders used today can effectively shoot in classroom or auditorium lighting, studio production picture quality can be improved with the use of additional lighting fixtures. Lighting the background and sets, as well as the talent, can add depth, color, and professionalism to your productions. Lighting can also be used to create an atmosphere or mood, establish a contrast between talent and sets, or evoke emotions in your audience.

Lighting Fixtures

One of the categories of lighting fixtures available today creates light using incandescent bulbs, which are filament bulbs, like the ones used in common household lamps. They can range in intensity from the small handheld battery pack models or camera-top mounted portable lamps to large strips of track lights mounted on the studio ceiling. These track lights, or strip lights, can often be fitted with plastic gelatins, or "gels," to provide color for background lighting effects (Figure 7.13).

Fig. 7.13. Track lights with barn doors.

Another category of studio lighting, and probably the most prevalent, uses tungsten halogen lamps. They are available in various wattages and often require the use of dimmers and scrims to adjust light brightness and temperature. Some models of halogen lamp lighting fixtures use a Fresnel lens to manipulate the concentration of light cast from the lamp. These lenses often have a control (wheel or joystick) on the back of the fixture that moves the lamp forward and back as the reflector changes the beam's focus from sharp to wide angle or diffused. Barn doors, small rectangular squares mounted on the front of the lens, can also be used to direct light where it is needed (Figure 7.14). These types of lighting devices fall into the category of focused lighting, because you can actually aim and focus the amount of light that you require for your subject. They come in a variety of sizes, from individual lamps to sets of lamp kits and stands. Still in the category of halogen lamps, one of the most popular studio lights is the scoop light (Figure 7.15). The scoop light is bowl shaped, large, and open in the front. There is also a control on the back of the scoop that allows adjustment to the focus of the light, from a narrow to a more diffused beam. Scoop lights are known as reflector lights, because the light is actually reflected and used to provide illumination over large areas of the production studio.

Fig. 7.14. A Fresnel light with barn doors.

Fig. 7.15. A scoop lighting fixture.

Another category of lighting fixtures that have recently become increasingly popular use fluorescent tubes as the lighting source (Figure 7.16). The tubes generate a large amount of diffused light without generating a lot of heat as the halogen bulbs tend to do. Also, recent innovations in the manufacturing of fluorescent bulbs has led to the development of full-spectrum lights. In the past, fluorescent bulbs cast a blue-tinted (color temperature) hue to the video image. The development of these full-spectrum bulbs has eliminated the problems usually associated with fluorescent lighting and video production.

Studio lighting fixtures tend to be controlled through the use of a lighting control board, or a least some type of control panel, commonly referred to as a dimmer pack. Use of a lighting control board enables the lighting director to set and control numerous lights at the same time, program different combinations of lights and light settings, and even set lighting times and sequence (Figure 7.17).

Fig. 7.16. A fluorescent lighting fixture provides illumination without excessive heat.

Fig. 7.17. A student adjusts studio lights using a dimmer control board.

Lighting Placement

Placement of light has a direct effect on how the video camera perceives a subject. Just putting lights "everywhere" creates a dull, flat, lifeless setting. Light placement and the correct combination of lighting is important for establishing a television production program. Four main functions of lighting need to be addressed:

- Key lighting, which focuses light on the subject
- Fill lighting, which fills in and removes shadows caused by the key light
- Backlighting, which separates the subject from the background and adds depth
- Background lighting, which illuminates the background area and sets

Even though there is no exact model for lighting, most lighting experts agree that the three-point model (key lights, fill lights, backlights) works well and provides an optimum lighting effect. First, let's look at the key light and its placement on the set.

As the name implies, the key light is the main light placed on the subject(s) of the program. In a studio setting, the key light is placed at an angle 30 to 45 degrees from the camera on either the left or right side. Elevation of the key light should also be set at a 45-degree angle. This will avoid shadow problems on the background or set, as well as having the brightness of the key light shining in the talent's eyes. Common choices for key lights generally involve focused light, such as the Fresnel lights.

The key light is the dominating light on the talent, creating form and dimension—and unfortunately shadows. The use of a fill light is necessary to remove the shadows by filling light in the shadowy areas created by the key light. To optimize lighting in the largest area possible, the fill light should be placed at a 90-degree angle from the key light and at 45-degree angle from the camera on the opposite side from the key light (Figure 7.18). This creates right angles from each of the lights to the subject area of the production. Elevation of the fill light is not as critical as that of the key light but should be enough to reduce shadows on the talent and set substantially. The required intensity of the fill light is less than that of the key light, providing a "softer" light to fill in shadows and provide some dimension to the camera. Some choices for appropriate fill lights include the use of scoops or even banks of color-balanced fluorescents.

The third lighting component involves the use of a backlight. The purpose of the backlight is to separate the subject from the background and provide depth and dimension in the shot. The backlight should be placed directly behind the subject but not on a direct horizontal line with the camera. This would reduce the camera's ability to pick up the subject distinctly from the background. The backlight needs to be elevated above the subject. A 45-degree angle is again most desirable. This will illuminate the subject without directly influencing the camera's ability to shoot. Backlight, like fill lights, should be softer (less wattage) than the key light. Finally, the background lights are added to light up the background sets (or curtains). They differ from the backlight, which is used to light the "back" of the subject, whereas background lights are used to light up the fronts of sets and backdrops. Almost any type of light can be used for background lighting, but it is important that the it meet these requirements:

Fig. 7.18. Three-point lighting diagram.

1. Background lights should not be stronger than the key light.

2. Background lights should be evenly distributed over the entire background that is visible on camera. There should be no distinct light and dark areas.

3. Background lights should not "hit" the subject area on the set.

Colored gels, scrims, and other diffusers are commonly used to provide illumination for backlighting and to avoid lighting problems that can occur on the rest of the set.

Fig. 7.19. Spotmeters allow for precise lighting measurements.

One of the best methods for testing and adjusting the lighting is to turn on the camera and view the lighting on a monitor as it will be seen by the viewer. It is even advisable to record some footage with and without talent to see how the lighted set appears on camera. Another ideal way to test the lighted set for "hot spots" (overlit areas) or dark zones (underlit areas) is to employ the use of a spotmeter. A spotmeter is a device that measures the intensity of reflected light, light that is being "bounced off" the subjects and backgrounds of a set. To measure the reflected light and find lighting problems, the spotmeter is held next to the camera lens and slowly panned across the set (Figure 7.19). The readings will indicate which, if any, portions of the set need to be adjusted in terms of lighting intensity. If readings are similar throughout the set, the lighting has been correctly placed and set.

Backdrops and Sets

Since the advent of television, the desire for a variety of sets and sophisticated backgrounds has grown with the available technology. Early sets consisted of curtains or painted backgrounds. Today's modern, sophisticated sets contain custom designed furniture, realistic backgrounds, electronic video screens and graphics, and even areas that are electronically composed and computer enhanced.

The size, shape, and design of your sets will depend on the focus and intent of the program, the size of the production studio, and the expertise and time allotments of the crew. Whether your set is simple or sophisticated, large or small, here are some simple rules to follow:

- The set and background only need to be as large as the area you are shooting. The height and width of the set doesn't need to be much taller than your subjects, nor wider than the props (desk, chairs, bookcases) it contains.

- Beware of contrast. Avoid high-contrasting colors and shades, such as black or white. Use pastels and shades of browns and grays. Avoid shiny, glossy surfaces and props that light up or sparkle.

- Remember, sets don't have to *be* real, they just have to *look* real!

- The talent should be level with the camera. If the program requires that talent and guests are seated, the set should be built on platforms and risers so that the camera is not "shooting down" on the subjects.

- Don't overshoot your talent. Just because you have a large background area, don't feel that you must feature it in every shot. Remember, the viewer is probably watching the program on a small monitor (19 to 36 inches). Feature the people, not the backgrounds. Start with a wide shot, then move in for close-ups and two shots.

Backgrounds for sets can be designed in a variety of ways. A popular and easy background is a cyc, or cyclorama (Figure 7.20), which is a set of canvas, cloth, or muslin curtains that are hung on tracks and used as backgrounds for studio sets and productions. Because they are on rollers, cycs can be easily pulled into place when needed. Some cycs are hung on multiple sets of tracks, so a combination of curtains (and colors) can be used at the same time.

Fig. 7.20. Cycs used for background during news show production.

Another type of background commonly used in television is a flat. Softwall flats are made from wooden frames (usually 1 inch thick) over which stretched muslin or canvas cloth is stapled or nailed into place (Figure 7.21). The cloth is then primed and painted. Painting can be done by set crews or even advanced art students, depending on the sophistication desired for the set. Some flats are simply solid colors, or a muted mixture of colors. Other flats can be done as murals of the school or community, scenes from nature, or any other pictorial relevant to the program. Hardwall flats can also be made from composition board, drywall, and even paneling nailed to frames of wood. Flats can be easily hung from the ceiling with the addition of cup hooks screwed into the top. Some programs have positioned them in place with stands and weights, much as a theater department would do for a play.

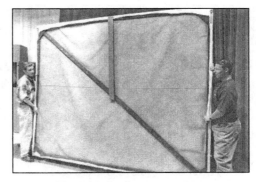

Fig. 7.21. Students prepare a softwall flat for production.

Murals and photographic backgrounds are readily available through the Internet, catalogs, and photography stores. They can range from a beautiful beach scene to a lighted city nightscape to a professional portrait backdrop. Some are expensive, but they can be placed on a flat wall or bulletin board to create a quick and easy backdrop.

Designing the set for a production can be fun—and challenging! Some considerations for set design include the following:

- **Budget constraints:** How much money is available for set design? Differentiate between "needed" items and "wanted" items. Which items can be found at no or low cost?

- **Time constraints:** How much time is allotted for set construction? Do you have time to build it, or must you buy it already constructed? Is there time to order items?

- **Usability constraints:** Will this set be used once, weekly, or every day? This determines construction and purchasing requirements.

The nature and content of the production will determine what kind of set is needed. For example, let's consider the production of a daily news as a typical school program. There are many styles of news shows on the market today. The local news show is probably still being produced and hosted by one to three anchors seated at a typical news anchor desk. The background, if there is one, may consist of hardwall flats, graphics, and maybe even a monitor or two for reporter segments. Building this kind of set would require little in terms of material, although construction of the desk might better be left to professional companies that specialize in furniture construction. The background flats and platforms (the talent is seated and should be raised to camera level) can be built by students in the television or theater program. Platform construction can consist of a frame constructed of posts made from 4" x 4" wood, framed with 2" x 2" wood, and flooring made with plywood. Exposed surfaces can be covered with indoor- outdoor carpeting (Figure 7.22).

Many news and entertainment programs use a "magazine"-style set instead of the traditional anchor desk. In this case, the host or hosts are standing rather than seated, and the set is more flamboyant than traditional news sets. There may be brighter colors painted on flats and furniture, use of creative props and eye-catching materials on the set, perhaps some active monitors, and even electronic graphics keyed in a chroma key screen area. Instead of an anchor desk, the hosts might be standing behind a counter or seated in front of a background on stools. A magazine-news show is more informal than a traditional news show, and the set and backgrounds should reflect that persona in their motif and style.

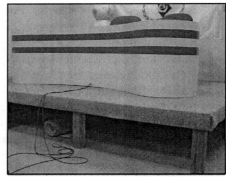

Fig. 7.22. Platforms are constructed to elevate sets and talent.

Producing the Program

Producing television programs is an exciting and challenging responsibility, involving a lot of creative and technical expertise. There is also a big emphasis on social and communication skills in working with both talent and crew. Producers have the responsibility to ensure that the program meets technical, creative, and budgetary standards. They must coordinate a variety of tasks from program conception to program completion.

Designing the Program

Television programs are produced to fulfill a need or interest of the viewing audience. Such programs can be as simple as those providing nightly entertainment or as complex as those identifying and solving national or community problems. If there is a lack of viewer interest in the topic, chances are the program will not be very successful. Citizens' concerns for the environment, for example, can serve as an impetus for creating programs about the environment and community action. Likewise, programs about school overcrowding, teacher shortages, college entrance exams, state-mandated grade changes, and other issues that directly affect students and teachers will be interesting to a viewing audience for a school-based production. Producers are constantly evaluating viewing needs and desires. Surveys, polls, and television rating companies are used to determine viewer interest and program demands. Producers must analyze collected data and use it to determine program content as well as program distribution.

Selecting the topic and designing the program is an important first step in television production. Next, the producers must consider the following factors before deciding if the show is feasible.

Time

Is there ample time to produce the program while the topic is currently on viewer's minds? For example, if student elections are being held next week, a producer would have to make a judgment as to whether there would be enough time to produce a program highlighting the candidates and issues. This type of program would not be feasible to produce if it could not be completed before the election is held.

Equipment and Expertise

Is there sufficient equipment available to produce the program? Are there enough qualified personnel to host and crew the production? A program on scuba diving would be great with shots from an underwater camera, but do you have one and someone who can dive and operate it? A comedy show about student life would be funny, but are there enough talented actors and writers to make it happen?

Budget Constraints

Will the cost of the program exceed the financial constraints of the project? Most programs have a limited budget allotment, and financial concerns are important when making production decisions. The producer must carefully estimate the cost of each program in terms of equipment, talent, production personnel, sets, props, and wardrobe.

Organizing the Program

Once a topic has been selected and approved, the producer must coordinate equipment, facilities, and personnel necessary for producing the project.

Production Personnel

The personnel needs of a program are dependent on the size and scope of the project or program. Naturally, the more sophisticated the program, the more personnel needed to operate equipment and provide on-air talent positions. Filling technical and talent positions should be done on the basis of expertise, experience, and availability. A list should be created identifying all possible tasks and positions needed to produce the program. Smaller productions or those on a limited budget often use one or two individuals to perform several tasks. In a school setting, it's important to utilize as many students as possible so they can gain experience and expertise with the equipment and techniques of studio production.

A studio production would include all or some of the following technical and talent positions:

- **Producer/Director:** In charge of coordinating and directing talent and production personnel
- **Technical director:** Operates the video mixer
- **Art director:** Designs and creates sets, displays, scenery, and props
- **Floor director:** Relays cues from the director to talent and studio personnel
- **Writer:** Transforms ideas into a written script
- **Audio engineer:** Sets up and operates audio equipment and sound sources
- **Videotape engineer:** Operates VCRs or other recording and playback equipment
- **Camera operator:** Operates the studio camera used for recording and broadcast

- **Graphics:** Designs and manipulates graphics during production
- **Lighting:** Sets up and operates lighting equipment
- **Talent:** Performs and acts on camera
- **Editor:** Edits recorded program material into finished master

The personnel needs of the program should be identified. Individuals should be selected based on expertise, experience, and availability. A list should be created identifying all possible tasks jobs that need to be filled (Figure 7.23).

After each position has been filled, the personnel should identify and secure their equipment and supplies. The lighting director, for example, may design and request several types of lights, fixtures, and colored gels for lighting the sets and talent. The audio engineer should identify microphone and other sound needs, such as music and sound effects. The graphics operator should design and create the necessary graphics for the program. These might include titles, keyed names for on-air personalities, and ending credits. Sets, props,

Fig. 7.23. Studio production involves both on-camera talent and technical personnel.

costumes, and accessories should be identified on a list and checked off as accumulated by the set director. Props for each scene should be stored together, perhaps in large boxes or crates clearly labeled with the program title and scene numbers. Sets need to be designed first on paper and then constructed and assembled in the studio. The producer and director need to conduct periodic meetings with cast and crew to determine progress, identify and solve problems, and maintain enthusiasm for the project.

Scheduling the Production

Production schedules are used to coordinate the activities of cast and crew, as well as expedite the completion of the project. They include locations, talent and crew information, as well as dates and times for rehearsals and production. They provide cast and crew the opportunity to plan and organize activities so everyone is prepared and ready for each production event. Last-minute problems (such as, "We don't have the . . .!") can be avoided by reviewing upcoming production activities with the responsible personnel. Production schedules should be posted and a copy given to each member of cast and crew.

A production schedule for a television program titled "Today's Schools: Protecting the Environment in Education" might look like this:

Show/Scene	Date/Time	Location	Talent/Crew
Opening/Closing	Aug. 21 1 PM–3 PM	Orlando High School Front entrance	John T., Reporter Crew 1
	Aug. 22 2 PM–3 PM	Orlando High School Dumpster area	John T., Reporter Interview with Mr. Nadel, Science Teacher Crew 2
Scene #2 Wastes	Aug. 23 12 PM–1 PM	Orlando High School Cafeteria	Jen W., Reporter Interview with Ms. Flint, manager Crew 2
Scene #3 Community Action	Aug. 25 3 PM–4 PM	Riverside High School Classroom 237 Environmental Club	Jen W., Reporter Interview with club president and club adviser Crew 1
Scene #4 County Effect	Aug. 28 5 PM–7 PM	School Office Third Floor	John T., Reporter Interview with Mr. Church Crew 1

This production schedule illustrates the planning and details necessary for completing television projects. The more complicated the production, the greater the need for organization and planning.

Recording the Production

Organizing and coordinating the efforts of cast and crew during production taping can be an exhilarating activity, and sometimes an exhaustive one, too. Delegate as many tasks and responsibilities as possible to responsible and reliable staff members. Delegating prevents the producer from becoming overwhelmed by the infinite number of small details involved in any studio production. The producer can assist in coordinating the various groups involved in the production by working closely with a few subordinates. Technical directors, floor directors, and even lighting directors can assist in maintaining momentum before, during, and after production. During the actual recording of program material, the producer can assist in directing talent and crew, offer suggestions for solving technical problems or improving technical quality, and solving any problems and concerns among the production staff.

Studio production likely involves the use of two or more video cameras. Placement of the cameras is important for optimizing camera angles and minimizing camera movement during the show (Figure 7.24). Studio cameras are often mounted on tripod dollies so they can be easily wheeled into position without much effort or noise. The camera placement and talent blocking is important to achieve good composition and keep the viewer oriented to the action in the scene. A crossing pattern is often used in situations in which there are two studio cameras. The camera on the left (Camera 1) should get the close-ups of the person on the right, and the camera on the right (Camera 2) should get the close-up of the person on the left. This approach will achieve the 45-degree profile desired for a talk show or other shows that feature a "host" and guests. The director may ask one of the cameras to "truck right" or "truck left" (a lateral movement of the camera) to obtain a wide-angle shot for instances when both actors are on camera (Figure 7.25). It is advisable to rehearse, if possible, camera movement and talent blocking (positions on stage) before beginning production. Clearly the camera operators and the director should be knowledgeable about the sequence and types of camera angles that will used during the course of the production. This information should be discussed during preproduction meetings with the studio crew.

Fig. 7.24. Camera placement is critical during studio production.

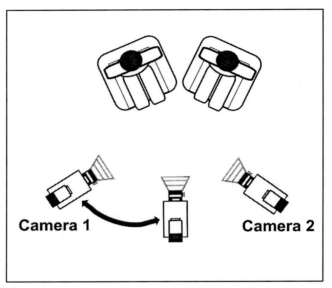

Fig. 7.25. Diagram indicates camera position and shot patterns for an interview program.

Keeping program segments and tapes organized is crucial when producing complex programs. Each tape should be clearly labeled and identified for editing purposes. There are often several "takes" for each program segment. A log can be kept with each tape identifying scene and take numbers.

Actual program recording should begin with 30 seconds of color bars accompanied by a 0-dB audio tone on all audio tracks. The color bars and tone, commonly referred to in the business as "bars and tone," are used for adjusting the monitors video and audio settings during playback. The bars and tone are followed by a recording of the slate, a small blackboard-like object, on camera. Today slates can also be electronically generated. The slate information contains the following:

- The title of the program
- Episode title and take number the date
- Audio information (mono, stereo, hi-fi, etc.)

Finally, add several seconds of black before you start recording the actual footage needed in the production. The producer should review each tape as soon as possible to check video and audio quality, as well as program continuity. Some producers will immediately rewind the tape following production and quickly check a few key points for quality and continuity.

Creating and producing television programs requires the talent of many individuals working together as a team to accomplish clearly stated production goals. Good studio projects don't just happen. They are carefully planned and scripted from beginning to end. Creativity and originality are traits that all producers should have to develop innovative and interesting programs for their viewing audience. Television producers take ideas and turn them into reality!

Review Questions

1. List and describe the three functions of a video mixer.

2. Define these video mixer components:

   Bus

   Bank

   Fader bar

   Preview bus

   Line-out

3. List four types of video sources that can be connected to video mixer for studio production.

4. What is the difference between a wipe and a dissolve?

5. Describe a production you have seen on network or cable television that used chroma key as an effect.

6. Briefly describe these DVE effects.

   Strobe

   Paint or posterization

   PIP (picture in a picture)

   Mosaic

7. Describe the function of each of these lighting techniques.

   Key light

   Fill light

   Backlight

   Background light

8. Describe how you would use each of these lights in a studio production.

   Scoop

   Fresnel

   Track Light

9. List and describe the three main components of a wired intercom system.

10. Describe how you would use a spotmeter to check the studio lighting on a set.

11. In set construction, what is a flat? List the two types of flats described in the chapter.

12. List and describe the three factors a producer should consider before beginning production on a program.

13. Describe how a teleprompter is designed and operated.

14. What is a slate? List the information contained on a slate.

15. What is a production schedule? Make a brief sample below. Be sure to clearly label each section and accurately complete the information needed.

Studio Project Plan: Studio Video

Topic: _____

Description of Completed Project

Students will become familiar with the planning, production, and postproduction aspects of a studio program. They will develop an understanding of the processes of production from conception to program completion. They will develop experience in coordinating both technical and on-camera skills to produce a 7- to 10-minute video project using studio equipment.

Format

1. Show opening: a video segment that must include the title of show, video footage, and an audio track. The show opening should not exceed 30 seconds.

2. Show content: script and topic to be determined by the cast and crew.

   • Topic must be approved by instructor.

   • Show must include at least two camera angles.

   • Script must be submitted for approval by instructor before production.

   • Graphics information such as facts and details about the topic or event (times or dates, statistical information) must be included within the show as well as beginning and ending credits.

   • A videotaped segment can be used within the show itself.

Personnel

Producer/director: _____

Selects cast and crew, assigns jobs, responsible for program development and completion of project, coordinates crew during production, creates production schedules.

Technical director: _____

Operates video mixer and assists in directing studio cameras and floor personnel.

Audio technician: _____

Sets up studio microphones, operates audio equipment, selects necessary music and sound effects, and assists in producing prerecorded segments.

Camera operators: _____

Assist in establishing camera shots and positions, operate the camera during taping, operate the camera for opening and internal video segments, cue talent, and relay director's cues to floor.

Videotape operators and editors: _____

Operate VCRs for recording and playback, cue tapes and segments, and edit opening and other necessary video segments, including final program.

Talent: _____

Writes script and is responsible for set, wardrobe, and props.

Notes

1. Start production on videotaped segments and show opening as soon as possible.

2. Keep it simple. Don't try to do too much too soon.

3. Meet as a team to review show progress, content, and production schedules.

4. Remember, this is a group effort. Everyone contributes to the success of the program.

Evaluation

The completed project will be worth 100 points.

- Show concept and content (25 points)
- Technical aspects (25 points)
- Format/production (25 points)
- Individual grade (job performance) (25 points)

Evaluation Sheet: Studio Video

Project Title: _____

Description of Program: _____

Personnel

Producer/director: _____

Technical director: _____

Audio technician: _____

Camera operator: _____

Graphics operator: _____

Videotape operator: _____

Talent: _____

Show content . . . . **(25 points)** _____

Topic and content appropriate for intended audience; informative, thorough presentation of subject matter.

Technical aspects . . . . **(25 points)** _____

Technically effective (video, sound, editing), camera placement and shots appropriate, program contains good continuity.

Format/Production . . . . **(25 points)** _____

Program format consistent with project plan; topic maintains viewer interest, length appropriate for subject matter.

Individual job performance . . . . **(25 points)** _____

Performed assigned tasks in timely and efficient manner; responsibly performed tasks related to job duty; teamwork.

Total Points Awarded . . . . **(Out of 100)** _____

Teacher Comments:

Student Project Plan: News Show

Description of Completed Project

Students will become familiar with the planning and production of a school news program. They will develop the concept, formulate the content, and define the format of the show. They will produce video clips and segments for use in a school news show. They will work as technical crew and cast to produce the finished program.

Format

1. The project will include a 30-second opening (video segment) that contains title graphics, video footage, and an audio track.

2. Some type of internal graphics are required within the news program. These can include, for example, names of anchors, graphic pictures displayed over anchor's shoulders, weather maps or weather information, sports or club calendars, or viewer information about event times and dates.

3. At least one voiceover with footage (anchor reads script while videotaped footage illustrating news item is displayed) that contains information about some aspect of student and school life or events.

4. At least one preproduced video segment using a switcher or that is edited in during postproduction must be included. These might include interviews, sports or school event highlights, an ENG report on some school/community topic, or even a commercial promotion for an upcoming club or school project or fundraiser.

5. Some school and community announcements should also be included in the show. These can include, for example, club meetings, senior graduation information, class information, or drama or theater auditions/plays.

6. Ending credits for the show should be included to provide the names and positions of all cast and crew members. This should be accompanied by an audio track.

Personnel

Producer/director: _____

Selects cast and crew, assigns jobs, responsible for program development and completion of project, coordinates crew during production, creates production schedules.

Technical director: _____

Operates video mixer and assists in directing studio cameras and floor personnel.

Audio technician: _____

Sets up studio microphones, operates audio equipment, selects necessary music and sound effects, and assists in producing prerecorded segments.

Camera operators: _____

Assist in establishing camera shots and positions, operate the camera during taping, operate camera for opening and internal (voiceover and ENG reports) video segments, cue talent, and relay director's cues to floor.

Videotape operators and editors: _____

Operate VCRs for recording and playback, cue tapes and segments, edit opening and other necessary video segments including final program.

Talent: _____

Writes script, acts as reporter on ENG project, and is responsible for set, wardrobe, and props.

Evaluation

The completed project will be worth 100 points.

- Show content (25 points)
- Technical aspects (25 points)
- Format/production (25 points)
- Individual grade (job performance) (25 points)

Evaluation Sheet: News Show

Project Title: _____

Description of Program: _____

Personnel

Producer/director: _____

Technical director: _____

Audio technician: _____

Camera operator: _____

Graphics operator: _____

Videotape operator: _____

Talent: _____

Show Content . . . . (25 points) _____

Topic and content appropriate for intended audience; informative, thorough presentation of subject matter.

Technical Aspects . . . . (25 points) _____

Technically effective (video, sound, editing), camera placement and shots appropriate, program contains good continuity.

Format/Production. . . . . (25 points) _____

Program format consistent with project plan; topic maintains viewer interest, length appropriate.

Individual Job Performance . . . . (25 points) _____

Performed assigned tasks in timely and efficient manner; responsibly performed tasks related to job duty; teamwork.

Total Points Awarded. . . . . (Out of 100) _____

Teacher Comments:

Studio Project: Teen Conflicts/Social Issues

Description of the Project

Students will present information about a social issue or conflict that affects teenager's lives today. Such issues could include balancing work and school, teen drivers, getting into college, making the right choices (drugs, alcohol, smoking), personal relationships, dating, student athletes and student scholars, and so on. The project should present opposing viewpoints of the issue (pros and cons) as well as provide facts and statistical information to reinforce each position.

Format

Project should include:

1. A 30-second opening containing video clips, title of show, and an audio track

2. At least one reporter with an ENG report to be rolled (edited) into the show

3. Graphics (internal) within the project showing statistical information

4. On-camera statements and opinions by people from both sides of the issue seated in the studio (much like a talk-show format, but with multiple guests and a host)

Method

1. Define the topic: _____

2. Define the pros and cons of the issue.

3. Research background information and statistics about your topic.

4. Produce an ENG report about the topic. This is to be rolled (edited) into the show during taping of the studio portion of the project.

5. Present various views and opinions on the topic in the show:

    • On-camera opinions from hosts and guests in studio

    • Interviews with professionals in the field on videotape

    • Videotaped comments from students and others on videotape rolled-in during studio portion of project

Personnel

Producer/director: _____

Technical director: _____

Audio technician: _____

Camera operator: _____

Graphics operator: _____

Videotape operator: _____

Talent (studio): _____ _____

ENG Reporter: _____

Evaluation

The completed project will be worth 100 points.

- Show concept and content (25 points)
- Technical aspects (25 points)
- Format/production (25 points)
- Individual job performance (25 points)

Evaluation Sheet: Teen Conflicts/Social Issues

Topic _____

Personnel

Producer/director: _____

Technical director: _____

Audio technician: _____

Camera operator: _____

Graphics operator: _____

Videotape operator: _____

Talent (studio): _____

ENG reporter: _____

Show content. . . . . (25 points) _____

Topic and content appropriate for intended audience; informative, thorough presentation of subject matter.

Technical aspects . . . . (25 points) _____

Technically effective (video, sound, editing), camera placement and shots appropriate, program contains good continuity.

Format/production . . . . (25 points) _____

Program format consistent with project plan; topic maintains viewer interest, length appropriate.

Individual grade (job performance) . (25 points) _____

Performed assigned tasks in timely and efficient manner; responsibly performed tasks related to job duty; teamwork.

Total Points Awarded. . . . . (Out of 100) _____

Teacher Comments:

Objectives

After successfully completing this lesson, you will be able to:

- use brainstorming approaches to develop movie ideas and concepts.
- develop a script for a video movie.
- create a storyboard for a video movie.
- create a plan to produce a video movie.
- identify logistics and locations for production of a video movie.

Vocabulary

audio track. The sound portion of a videotape.

complexity. The use of a variety of camera angles and editing to enhance the intensity of action in a scene.

continuity. Preserving the visual coherence and perceived reality of an event.

cutaway shot. Video shot used to intercut between two shots to avoid jump cuts and continuity problems.

establishing shot. Video shot used early in the sequence to identify the setting for the following action. Establishes time and location of the scene for the audience.

jump cut. An awkward shift in continuity when two scenes are linked too abruptly during either videotaping or editing.

postproduction. Video editing, sound mixing, and the addition of titles and graphics to produce a completed project or program.

props. Objects used in the scene either by actors or as part of the set design.

storyboarding. The process of planning a video project that includes drawing a simple sketch of the desired shot, planning the accompanying audio, and estimating the duration of each element of the paragraph.

treatment. A brief description of a film topic or idea.

wild sound. Random sounds recorded on location to add to the soundtrack to add ambience and realism.

Up to this point, this text has focused on nonfiction television with an emphasis on learning to use video production equipment in a school setting. Producing short video reports, documentaries, and certain studio productions is an excellent way to learn the skills of television production, but creating entertaining fictional programs can also be educational and fun as well. This chapter covers the planning and production of video movies. These movies can be used to creatively illustrate concepts in the school setting (lab safety, for example), develop the talents of students in the theater and video program for work in the industry, or to use as an entry in a video contest.

Just how are successful projects created? Good fiction television, just like good nonfiction television, is the result of careful planning and detailed production.

Preproduction: Before You Shoot

As you probably know by now, a large portion of the work on any video project is done before the camera begins recording the first frame. Preproduction of a video movie involves the development of the topic or concept, logistical considerations, scripting, storyboarding, and planning the actual shoot.

Topic Development

How are the ideas and concepts developed for movies? Where do they come up with all the ideas for movies in the theater and on the television screen?

Movie ideas can often come from other literary forms: books and novels, short stories, poems, and even songs. The process of creating a movie by adapting a story from another literary source is a well-documented and accepted practice. Developing story ideas by adapting an idea or concept from another source nonetheless requires creativity and imagination.

Here is an example: a student crew adapted the story "Little Red Riding Hood" from the traditional tale of a little girl walking through the woods to visit her sick grandmother and being confronted with a mean wolf into a modern tale of a young woman traveling across a crowded urban city to visit her invalid grandmother while being stalked by a pedophile. The inspiration for this idea came from listening to a song on the radio, "Little Red Riding Hood," and using the original story as the vehicle for this adaptive tale.

Another way to generate ideas for a video movie is brainstorming. Just about everyone has an idea for a movie, whether it's a drama or a comedy, maybe even an action adventure. Brainstorming is the process of listing ideas that come up through an open discussion. Each idea is listed on a large board or poster as it is suggested during the discussion. Some class members will begin to combine and improve on the submitted ideas. Usually within a short period of time, a topic emerges that combines the most exciting elements of many of the ideas. Here's an example of how brainstorming works: One idea submitted by a high school student involved a young man visiting New York City and meeting many types of people on the streets of the city. Another student wanted to add a mystical aspect, and still another wanted to parody a Hollywood classic. Many other students wanted to explore the restlessness that many teenagers experience. After some discussion, the group decided to produce a video short about a restless, underachieving youth who is dissatisfied with his job (delivering chicken on a bicycle) and his surroundings (overbearing mother and bullying neighborhood kids). Through a freak accident, the young man is magically transported to New York City. He meets many interesting characters as he tries to find his way home. He must finally confront a bully and soon gains his dignity and self-respect. He also learns, like Dorothy in the *Wizard of Oz*, that there's no place like home. In fact, the title of this movie turned out to be *No Place Like Home*. Any one of the ideas presented by a group member probably could have made a passable project, but using brainstorming to combine ideas and elements brings a complexity and depth to the video project that might not have occurred if ideas were not discussed in an open forum (Figure 8.1).

The idea or concept of your movie, when developed, is called a treatment, which is basically a few sentences that tell what your movie will be about. Developing the treatment is the first step in the process of producing a video movie.

Logistical Considerations

Most school production teams are limited in their locations and budgets for short fictional video programs. Your group's best idea may be a story of international intrigue set on a navy battleship in the middle of the ocean. However, unless you live near a shipyard and your uncle is one of the Joint Chiefs of Staff, you may

Fig. 8.1. A teacher leads a student brainstorming session.

have some difficulty with the setting of your video. If you live in Iowa, a program about a surfing champion may be out of reach. Think about the locations and resources near your school and within your community. A story about a homeless person befriended by a caring group of school children works well if you live in an urban community. There are plenty of locations available for busy street shots and deserted alleys. If you live in a rural setting, the story may have to be changed to a homeless wanderer befriended by a local farmer or rancher.

Certainly careful set building can overcome some logistical problems. But remember, people expect more accuracy and authenticity from television than they do from a play. Many high school thespian groups have presented the musical *Oklahoma!* The set usually consists of a makeshift farmhouse façade, a few bales of hay, and perhaps even a few stalks of corn in ceramic pots and a clothesline full of quilts and flannel shirts. The audience is willing to suspend its disbelief and imagine they are in nineteenth-century Oklahoma. The audience would be much less willing to play along with the same setting on the television screen, however. Television viewers have come to expect accuracy in location and setting. Building elaborate sets is also costly and time-consuming, two factors that make it prohibitive in school video programs. This is why using locations and natural features of your community make much more sense.

Scouting locations for scenes in your video movie is important for developing the script and storyboards that will come later in the project. There are several things you can do to make the task of finding locations successful and beneficial to the production of your movie.

1. Make a list of the scenes in your movie. Imagine the setting of each scene and write a brief description of where you depict the action would occur.

    Example:
    Scene 1: John is delivering chicken on his bicycle and confronted by neighborhood bullies.
    Location: Residential neighborhood or apartment community

2. Take pictures of each location with a digital or 35mm camera. Include some wide-angle shots as well as medium and close-ups to show details. These are great to take back to the production crew to share your location ideas with the entire crew. These photographs are also helpful when completing storyboards for the actual production (Figure 8.2).

Fig. 8.2. Digital cameras are ideal for scouting and sharing shooting locations.

3.   Take along several copies of a letter on school letterhead (signed by your teacher) that explains what you are doing (scouting locations for a school movie production) and contact information (school name and phone numbers) in case there are any questions or concerns if someone questions you about your actions. A group of teens walking around taking pictures on public or private property has the potential to raise some eyebrows. It is also helpful to have the letter in case you wish to use some interior scenes—inside a store or restaurant, for example. Most businesses are willing to oblige a school production but might be hesitant to allow access to a group of teenagers with no affiliation to an educational institution.

4.   Take along a detailed city or county map. Clearly label and mark the locations you find acceptable on the map. This will help the producer when it comes time to make a production schedule. Knowing the distance and routes the crew must take can assist in planning location shoots, dates, and times. It can also prevent crews from getting "lost" and wasting valuable production time.

Obviously, budget requirements must be considered in school video production. Decide early how much money you can spend on the project. You may want to begin your video with an aerial shot of a city park, but unless the footage already exists and is available to you or you can get a helicopter service to donate some time for your production, this shot may be out of reach. A big budget is not a requirement for a successful program. Take careful stock of your resources—the availability of funds and ways to generate funds—and plan accordingly.

Scripting

Once you have fine-tuned the concept of your program and solved any serious logistical problems, you can begin writing your script. Like a research paper or any other school paper, writing a script is easier if you can work from an outline. Knowing what characters will be in each scene, the action that will occur, and even the location of the scene can expedite the scriptwriting immensely. Create this outline, scene by scene, before you even begin writing the script.

When creating the script, try to write in a conversational style. The spoken word is much different from the written word. Read each line of dialogue after you have written it. Close your eyes and try to imagine your character saying the line. An escaped convict probably would not use the same words as a college professor. Try to get a feel for the type of language used by each character in your production.

Stage directions should also be included in the script. Stage directions describe the physical actions of the actors in the program as they are saying the lines.

Example:

John (*Struggling to peddle bike uphill*): "There has got to be a better way to make money than peddling chicken up and down the block."

> *A car (convertible) pulls alongside John. There are four teens in the car leering at John.*

Bully 1 (*driver of car, mocking voice*): "Hey John, let's hear you do the Colonel Cluck!"

Bully's Girlfriend (*Places hands under her arms imitating a chicken*): "Cluck, Cluck, Cluck!"

John (*Peddles faster, nervously looking over shoulder*): "Leave me alone. Can't you find someone else to annoy? I have work to do!"

As you can see from this example, stage directions can convey actions (*Places hands under her arms*) by the characters as well as emotions (*mocking voice*). They are helpful to both the cast and the crew in facilitating production. Stage directions (describing the physical actions of characters) can also be crucial to the plot. In the example, John's actions (*peddles faster and looks nervously over his shoulder*) will eventually lead to him crashing his bike and waking up in the streets of New York City. Stage directions act as cues for both talent and director and serve to maintain the scriptwriter's interpretation of the scene. They also give a concrete picture of what would be an abstract design of dialogue on paper.

Just as you describe the actions and emotions of your actors, it can also be helpful to include some basic descriptions of your characters and the setting. This is especially true early in a scene or if a character's appearance changes in the course of the program. Even some basic camera angles and shots can be included to give additional conceptual information to cast and crew. Most scenes begin with an *establishing shot* that gives the viewer some information about the setting. For example, in the previous scene:

Setting: Quiet residential area, late afternoon. Bike and rider are seen struggling to peddle up a hill.

> *Camera cuts from long establishing shot to medium shot looking at front of bike. John is wearing a red cap with a rubber chicken mounted on top. He has on a white shirt, a red bow tie, and black pants. His face is covered with sweat.*

Describing the setting, the characters in each scene, and some establishing shots and camera angles can improve and enhance the scriptwriting process. Cast and crew can begin to imagine the story, scenes, and characters as they will appear in the movie.

The process of scriptwriting is the next essential step in the preproduction phase of moviemaking. Scripts often go through many drafts and revisions before the final copy is approved. Have the actors and actresses read their lines in character. Sometimes they will have some insightful ideas to add to the story line or dialogue. The director and videographers can also be helpful in describing possible camera shots and angles to establish scenes in the story.

Storyboarding

Once the script has been finalized, it is time to develop the storyboards that will be used to create the visual representation of camera shots and angles during the production. A storyboard includes the drawing of a camera shot (and usually a description of the shot), the audio portion of the scene (usually dialogue), and the length or time of the shot (Figure 8.3). Storyboarding a fiction short is somewhat more difficult than storyboarding an ENG report or a documentary. Depending on the videography skills of the camera crew and the editing capabilities in postproduction, each scene will have many camera angles and locations to include in the finished storyboards. Try to storyboard as many camera angles as possible without distracting from the script.

Let's say, for example, that the first scene is a one-minute conversation between a teenage boy and girl in a high school cafeteria. The entire scene could be storyboarded as a single medium two-shot of both the boy and the girl standing there and talking. Shot in this way, after a few seconds, the scene would be boring and uninteresting to the viewers watching this single camera angle. To enhance the scene, read the script closely and plan additional camera angles such as close-ups, reaction shots, over-the-shoulder shots, and a point of view shot as the scene ends and the boy is watching the girl storm out the door (Figure 8.4). This adds complexity to the scene and creates a more dynamic video to interest viewers. Complexity is created through the use of a variety of closer camera angles and frequent camera-angle changes. The more angles used in a scene, the more exciting the pace of the scene and program. For a one-minute conversation, six or eight camera angles and changes would suffice. For a one-minute chase or fight scene, you may want to storyboard 15 to 20 shots.

Storyboard

Project _____ **Page**_____ **of**_____

Visual	Audio	Time
_____ _____		_____ _____
_____ _____		_____ _____
_____ _____		_____ _____

Fig. 8.3. Sample storyboard.

Visual	Times	Audio
 Medium 2-shot of boy and girl in cafeteria	0:00 — 0:06	"It's about time you showed up. I've been standing here like an idiot for the last ten minutes."
 Close-up of girl (mockingly)	0:06 — 0:10	"That's nothing new."
 Close-up of boy (angry)	0:10 — 0:14	"Oh, is that supposed to be funny?"

Fig. 8.4. Storyboard example.

Storyboarding also assists in avoiding continuity effects in both production and postproduction. Jump cuts are a good example. A jump cut occurs when two scenes are shot or edited together and the actions of the actors seemingly "jump" from one position to another. Storyboarding the shot sequences can avoid these mistakes by including cutaway shots in the sequences. Cutaway shots are shots that literally cutaway from the main action but show a related subject or a separate action that is going on at the same time. Some producers will actually plan and shoot their cutaway shots before recording their scenes. Let's go back to our scene in the cafeteria with the boy and girl and look at some cutaway shots that could be included in that scene. The main action occurring on camera is the conversation between the boy and the girl, mostly close-ups, medium shots, and some over-the-shoulder shots. Perhaps there is a distinct shift in the positions of the boy and girl during taping, and when one close-up of the boy is edited to the next over-the-shoulder shot of the girl, there is a drastic shift in the boy's body position. This would result in a jump cut, so a cutaway shot is inserted between the close-up and the over-the-shoulder shot. Possible cutaways for this scene could include the following:

- Cafeteria workers serving food look up, surprised by the commotion in the room.

- Girls seated at a table near the two students point and giggle at the obvious disagreement between the couple.

- A lunchroom monitor creases his brow and starts toward the arguing couple.

- A crowd of students begins to gather as onlookers to the action.

These shots would be recorded and canned for later use during postproduction. If needed, a couple of seconds of the shot would be inserted to avoid continuity problems in a scene.

The storyboard is a living document—changeable and adaptable. If you formulate a change of scene during production, don't be afraid to tape it both ways. Just make notes on the storyboard so the editor can decide which results were better and should be used during postproduction.

Storyboarding is a task performed best by individuals or a small group. The storyboards and visuals need to be consistent from the first to the last scene. The visual style and feel of a movie is created during the storyboarding phase, and all the scenes in the movie should be similarly planned, shot, and recorded for continuity. Certain scenes can be assigned to individuals or small groups who are interested in storyboarding, can interpret the script into visuals, and have some concept for camera shots and angles. In a school setting, an ideal team for storyboarding can be composed by pairing one or two television production students with students in the art program. The television students can assist in describing the shots and angles, the art students are proficient at drawing them. This has worked well for several schools and programs.

Planning the Production

Once the script and storyboards have been completed, it is time to plan and organize the production and recording of the scenes. The concept and development of a production schedule was discussed and explained in Chapter 7, "Studio Production." Similarly, the development of a production schedule will also be useful for planning and organizing the production sequences for your movie. Some important aspects to consider follow.

Times and Dates

Establish times and dates that will work best for your project. Make sure to consider the continuity of the project, especially if you are shooting in different locations or on different days. For example, let's imagine a video in which a young man gets off work in the early evening and rides the city bus home. Scene 1 shows the young man packing papers into a briefcase at his office desk and getting on an elevator. Scene 2 shows him exiting a high-rise office building and boarding a city bus on the street corner as dusk gives way to evening. Scene 3 shows the young man disembarking the city bus and walking down the street to his apartment building. If no windows or outside doors are shown in Scene 1 (office interior), this scene can be shot at any time of the day. Scene 2 (exiting building and boarding city bus) must be shot in the early evening and must coincide with the city bus schedule. Now, when does Scene 3 (apartment exterior) need to be scheduled? In the evening. Shooting Scene 3 (apartment exterior) in the morning would lead the viewer to believe that the young man had ridden the city bus all night! This wouldn't be logical, because commuting office workers and city buses do not travel all night from home to work locations.

The shooting schedule for this production might look like this:

Day/Time	*Scene*	*Location*	*Crew*
Mon. 1/12, 3 PM	Scene 1	Office Building/ Downtown	Team 1
Mon. 1/12, 5:30 PM	Scene 2	Downtown/Bus Station	Team 1
Tues. 1/13 5:30 PM	Scene 3	Apartments	Team 1

In this example, both Scene 1 and Scene 2 can be shot on the same day. There would most likely not be enough time to travel to the Scene 3 location and shoot Scene 3 on Monday. Therefore, production on Scene 3 would occur the next day so that the time continuity in the scenes would occur.

Once each scene is scheduled, make a list of all the talent and technical crew needed for each scene. Only those needed for each scene should be required to attend the production. It is not effective to have everyone involved in the movie present for every scene. Many producers will divide and assign their cast and crew to production "teams" or "crews." This makes it easy to identify which personnel will be working on each scene. Allow plenty of time for the production of each scene. Be sure to consider equipment setup time as well as time allotted for packing and travel from scene to scene. Rushed work is seldom professional and leaves a lot of margin for mistakes. Be sure a large copy of the production schedule is posted and that every cast and crew member receives an individual copy.

Scouting the Location

A crew should never arrive at a location cold, that is, with no idea of the layout and available facilities (parking, changing rooms, restrooms, power plugs, lighting, etc.). There are many factors that need to be considered in choosing and working at a location outside the school's facility. Once locations have been chosen, a crew member(s) should be sent out with a Location Fact Sheet (Figure 8.5). The sheet can be completed at the scene and duplicated for consideration by the production crew prior to shooting at that scene.

Equipment

The worst-case scenario is that everyone arrives at the location of the shoot and an integral piece of equipment is missing or forgotten back at the studio. Complete an Equipment Checklist (Figure 8.6) for each location you are using. The list of needed items is checked by the person in charge of production for the scene, usually the director or producer. As each item is packed in the studio for transport, it is checked in the "out" column. At the end of the day's production, the equipment is returned to the studio and the "returned" column is checked. In this manner, equipment is neither forgotten nor lost.

LOCATION FACT SHEET

PRODUCTION _____ No. _____ DATE _____

LOCATION NAME	LOCATION	CONTRACT
SCENE NUMBERS	ADDRESS	ADDRESS

 # pages ____ ☐ day ☐ int ☐ night ☐ ext | PHONE | PHONE

AVAILABILITY (times & days)

# DAYS NEEDED Prep: Shoot: Wrap:	Date Needed	Date Secured

DISTANCE FROM PRODUCTION OFFICE miles ____ minutes ____

SECURED
☐ contract
☐ copy filed

☐ insurance
☐ copy filed
☐ key
☐ extra key

SUPPORT NEEDS
☐ police
☐ fire department
☐ guards

FACILITIES   LOCATION
☐ rest rooms
☐ eating area
☐ make up
☐ wardrobe
☐ actor's area
☐ secure storage
☐ prod. staff area
☐ equipment area

PARKING   LOCATION
☐ grip truck
☐ camera truck
☐ campers
☐ staff cars
☐ picture cars
☐ generator
☐ vans (props, sound, etc.)

DESCRIPTION OF LOCATION

☐ size of access door: _____ ceiling ht: _____
☐ wall finishes:
☐ ceiling:
☐ floor:
☐ natural light:

☐ practicals:

ELECTRICAL DISTRIBUTION
☐ box available   phase _____
    circuits _____ amps _____ volts _____
    distance from set _____ ft.
☐ meter loop needed   ☐ installed
    phase _____ amps _____ volts _____
    distance from set _____ ft.
    from loop to transformer _____ ft.
☐ Are room outlets grounded? (YES) (NO)

SOUND ENVIRONMENT

WRAP PLANS

SPECIAL PROBLEMS/ LIMITATIONS

REQUIRED CONSTRUCTION/SET DRESSING

☐ ROOM PLAN on back   indicate compass   LOCATION MANAGER: _____

☐ route map ON BACK   direction on both   LOCATION SCOUT: _____

Fig. 8.5. Location Fact Sheet.

Equipment Checklist

Program Title: _____

Scene: _____ Location: _____

Item	Date Needed	Date Out	Date Returned
Camcorder	/ /	/ /	/ /
Tapes	/ /	/ /	/ /
Tripod	/ /	/ /	/ /
Microphone—handheld	/ /	/ /	/ /
Microphone—lavaliere	/ /	/ /	/ /
Microphone—shotgun	/ /	/ /	/ /
Microphone: _____	/ /	/ /	/ /
Lighting: _____	/ /	/ /	/ /
_____	/ /	/ /	/ /
Monitor(s): _____	/ /	/ /	/ /
_____	/ /	/ /	/ /
Headphones: _____	/ /	/ /	/ /
Other: _____	/ /	/ /	/ /
_____	/ /	/ /	/ /
_____	/ /	/ /	/ /
_____	/ /	/ /	/ /
_____	/ /	/ /	/ /
_____	/ /	/ /	/ /

Fig. 8.6. Equipment Checklist.

Costumes and Props

It is highly recommended that one or two persons be responsible for selecting, collecting, and dispensing the necessary costumes and props for the production. The wardrobes of the talent should be considered first. What each actor will wear for each scene should be listed on a Wardrobe and Prop Sheet (Figure 8.7) and checked off as it is acquired. Here's an example:

Scene	Character	Wardrobe Items (Check when acquired)	Props (Check when acquired)
Scene 1	John	Suit __ Shirt __ Tie __ Socks ___ Dress shoes ___	Briefcase ___ Papers/folders ___ Wallet ___ Bus ticket ___

Clothing and costumes (if needed) should be gathered and hung in the studio (dry cleaners can provide bags) and labeled with the character's name and scene identification on the outside of the bag. As props and wardrobe are collected, they can be checked off the list. As each scene is shot, the wardrobe can be returned to the same bag for storage and use in the next scene or scenes.

Props should also be stored by scenes and placed in boxes or paper grocery bags clearly labeled on the outside. When a scene is completed, the props should be neatly returned to the prop boxes or bags. Occasionally a scene may have to be reshot days or even weeks after production has been completed. It is advisable to keep all props and wardrobe complete until the program has been deemed "completed."

Expect the Unexpected

Part of the excitement of video production is the range of factors that just cannot be controlled. Most things that cannot be controlled can at least be anticipated!

- Bring backup equipment just in case—a camera, microphone, or another piece of essential equipment malfunctions. Think, "What can we not do *without*?"

- Plan for changes or extremes in weather. What if it rains? Have some clean, empty garbage bags handy, not only to protect equipment, but to make fast and easy ponchos for crew members.

- Plan for substitute crew members in case someone is absent due to illness. Be sure everyone has a list of telephone numbers to call in an emergency to find a substitute, if needed.

- Make sure that you are able to control your environment to create your scene. For example, one group planned to shoot a scene in which a bully tips over a garbage can in a city park. Everything went fine until the team realized that the garbage cans were bolted to the cement! A team member had to rush to the hardware store and buy a garbage can along with a bag of potting soil. A few of the team members busily dented the shiny garbage can and smeared it with the black dirt, while the other students searched for garbage (hitting pay dirt in their instructor's car!). The lesson from all of this? Don't assume anything!

Wardrobe and Prop Sheet

Wardrobe Manager _____ **Prop Manager** _____

Scene #	Character	Wardrobe Items (check when acquired)	Props (check when acquired)

Fig. 8.7. Wardrobe and Prop Sheet.

• Be prepared for hungry and thirsty crewmembers. Production time often interferes with lunch and dinnertimes. It is not always possible, or feasible, to halt production so everyone can go to a nearby (if there is one) fast-food restaurant for food and drink. Bring a few boxes of granola bars, fruit, muffins, crackers, cookies, and a cooler full of drinking water to your locations. This will save production time and keep the smiles on the cast and crew.

Production

When all of your preproduction activities have been completed, you are ready to begin shooting the scenes for your movie.

Videotaping the Scenes

Camcorder

Check the settings on your camcorder before you begin rolling tape for any scenes. Is the white balance setting correct (indoor, outdoor), or are you manually white-balancing for each scene and location? What about the focus setting? The setting should be set on manual so the camera's autofocus mechanism will not adjust the focus during taping (which sometimes causes brief "out of focus" footage). Be sure to roll tape before and after each shot or scene for at least 5 to 10 seconds. This will prevent an accidental erasure or taping over of footage from one scene to the next, especially if scenes are replayed and previewed after each taping. Allowing time and space between scenes prevents mistakes and will assist in the postproduction and editing process.

Shoot what you think you need, then shoot some more "just in case." Earlier in the chapter, the concept of cutaway shots was discussed. While videotaping the scenes, include at least two takes of each scene and several cutaways to be used in case there are some continuity problems in the scenes. Shooting several takes of each scene enables the director (and editor) to select the scene with the best angles, sound, and acting instead of being provided with a choice of this or nothing. Shooting cutaways is always a good idea because you never know when you might need them, and it is almost impossible to recreate them once the production is over.

While shooting scenes at the location, it is logical to record several minutes of footage containing wild or ambient sound that may be used in the audio portion of the postproduction. For example, if the scene takes place in an inner-city alleyway, take the camera to a nearby busy street and record several uninterrupted minutes of the sounds of traffic and other city noises (pedestrians, horns honking, sirens). If the location is in a city park, recording several minutes of park noises (birds chirping, children playing, visitors walking and talking) would be useful to the postproduction editor. Real-life ambient sound is always preferable to using prerecorded sound effects available on CD (Figure 8.8).

Monitor

It is not essential, but highly preferable, to bring along a color monitor (10 to 13 inch) to the shoot. A color monitor can be used to establish the camera framing by allowing the director and videographer to see the picture being recorded without

Fig. 8.8. A videographer records wild or ambient sound (traffic) for postproduction.

having to both peer into a small viewfinder or LCD panel. A color monitor will also be invaluable during scene playbacks. The cast and crew can easily view the recorded footage and if needed, make adjustments to camera angles or talent blocking for reshoots (Figure 8.9).

Storyboards

Even though you've been laboring over the project for weeks, don't forget to bring along the storyboards for each scene you are taping. Unless an emergency presents itself, stick to the storyboards. Load the storyboards into clear plastic sheet protectors and place them in a three-ring binder. The storyboards should be consulted before each camera angle is created. Adjustments to camera angles and script at the scene can be written on the plastic with a marker or vis-à-vis pen, which can be erased with a cloth or towel, for postproduction.

Fig. 8.9. A production team ensures picture quality and composition with the use of a color monitor at the location.

Rest

If you have several scenes to videotape on one day, encourage cast and crew members to rest whenever possible. Movie production is exciting, even on the high school level. Make sure team members do not get burned out by 10:00 A.M. during an all-day shoot. Pace the production so that there are rest periods for cast and technical crewmembers whenever possible.

Teamwork

The day of the shooting is not the time to question the director about the content and technique of the script or storyboards. If they have been carefully scripted and planned, the cast and crew should be prepared for the shoot. At the location, it is time to get the job done. There is a thin line between being creative and trying to commandeer the production. Every team member should be on the same page. Put aside egos, shelve personal agendas, and work for the good of the team. Avoid confrontations, derisive remarks, or comments that offend members of cast and crew. Keep your mind on your task and a smile on your face.

Labeling and Logging Recorded Material

Fig. 8.10. Tape appropriately labeled with scene and take numbers.

Even if the crew shoots the best video footage for the movie, it will be of little use in postproduction if you can't locate the desired takes and scenes. For this reason, recorded material should be carefully labeled and logged as it is used in the production. Information on the label should include scene number, take numbers, and times (see Figure 8.10).

During production, a tape log (Figure 8.11) can be used to record tape and scene numbers as well as other information important to the editor during postproduction. When tapes are previewed, crew members can make notes on the log concerning which takes were best, which will speed up the editing process.

Don't forget to pull out the videotape's erase tab to avoid reusing and accidentally erasing footage during the shoots.

Video Tape Log

Project _____ **Date** _____

Tape #	Scene #	Scene	Location	Storyboard Pages	# of Takes

Fig. 8.11. Video tape log.

Postproduction: The Finishing Touch

You can produce a professional video project by employing appropriate audio and video editing techniques. Here are some ideas that should help you with the moviemaking process.

Viewing and Evaluating Raw Footage

The first step in postproduction is viewing and evaluating the raw footage shot on location. Assuming that you have viewed the raw footage at the location, viewing and evaluating footage in the studio becomes an exercise in judgment and selection of the best takes. Carefully examine each take to determine which one to use in the finished project. Several team members (videographer, director, editor) should view the raw footage because each person will see different aspects in the shot. Indicate on the tape log which takes for each scene are preferable and should be used during the editing process (Figure 8.12). This will simplify the decision-making process during postproduction, speeding up the process. Once all scenes have been previewed and identified, you are ready to edit.

Fig. 8.12. Production crew previews raw footage.

Videotape Editing

The editor should begin editing the tape with at least 30 seconds of color bars and an 0-dB audio signal on all audio tracks. This is then followed by 10 to 15 seconds of black. The bars and tone will assist in adjusting the playback monitors when the project is viewed or for duplicating purposes.

As for the project itself, the editor should be provided with the completed storyboards, tape logs, and director's notes for each scene. At the point of editing, the creative process is over, and the editor is simply combining the shots in sequence as described in the storyboards and notes. Although editing is creative, it is a reflection of the planning of the project. The editor should craft the raw footage into a complete program, rather than attempt to salvage poorly planned and poorly executed scenes.

Remember the basic concepts of editing (refer to Chapter 6). Quick edits can make a scene more exciting and intense. Longer edits of carefully chosen scenes can provoke thought and introspection in your audience. Apply a simple rule to your program pace: Whether the pace is fast or slow, the program should never be difficult to watch. Unlike your team, the audience will have no idea of the excitement to come. The audience lives in the moment of the picture on the screen. The program should be captivating from start to finish. Don't make the audience wait for "the good part." There is no guarantee that the audience will be there when it finally arrives.

Review the edited material often. Once a scene has been completed, take the time to watch the finished version before moving on to the next scene. Have another crewmember (videographer or director) watch the scene for continuity and effect. It is always easier to make changes and adapt the scene earlier in the editing process rather than later.

Audio Editing

As described in earlier chapters, music and sound effects can be added to your program; sometimes their careful selection can make or break your final product. If your movie requires a music soundtrack to carry the action or scene or as background to dialogue some considerations must be made.

1. The tempo and tone of the music should reflect the pace of the movie. The music should reflect the mood and tone of the video.

2. Music can be used to enhance the setting of the story. A scene that is set in 1956 would best be served by music of that era.

3. Avoid making your project into a music video. The soundtrack enhances the overall project but should not be the main focus of the project. Avoid long scenes with little or no dialogue that contain only a music soundtrack.

4. Consider purchasing prerecorded production music to use in your projects. Production music can offer you the music you need to set the mood and retain the copyright for your production. This is especially true in projects that are to be entered into video contests and for later duplication to cast and crew members. Production music can be purchased from a number of music companies or produced in your school's music lab (Figure 8.13).

Fig. 8.13. Production or royalty-free music is recommended for student video projects.

Sound effects can be very effective in movies. Creative use of simple sound effects can enhance both the mood and the action of the scene. For example, in a short comedy movie, a young man takes a bite of a sandwich, then faces the camera (close-up) with a rather unpleasant expression. To magnify his reaction to the unpleasant taste, the crew went to the orchestra room and recorded a percussionist playing a rising note on a timpani ("boing"). This sound effect was then edited into the scene as an audio exclamation point. The audience was treated to a visual (facial expression) as well as an audio ("boing") cue in the action.

Another student crew taping an action scene made creative use of some sound effects to enhance the comedic aspects of their video. In their scene, a young man is confronted by a street bully. The bully extorts money from the young man, who has finally decided that enough is enough. As the bully walks away laughing, the young man picks up a tin can from the sidewalk and hurls it at the bully, hitting him in the back of the head. A sound effect ("plunk") made from a hollow wood block being struck with a wooden mallet, was added as the can strikes the bully's "hollow" head. Then as the bully turns to face the young man, smoke comes from his ear's (blown through plastic tubes taped behind his ears) and the sound of a train whistle is added. When the bully charges the young man for revenge, the sound of a locomotive accelerating is used. The young man picks up two garbage can lids and makes a bully-lid sandwich. A cymbal crash was added to provide a sound effect for this shot. The shot then switches to a close-up of the dazed bully in profile, stumbling backward and falling to the pavement. A metallic note is played and modulated with an electric keyboard ("wah-wah"), giving a cartoon-like appeal to this potentially violent scene. The enhancement of the comedic overtones through the use of the various sound effects was very effective and provided laughs for the audience.

Ambient or wild sound can also be used to enhance the mood and realism of the video movie. Earlier in the chapter, we recommended that the videographer record several minutes of uninterrupted footage containing the ambient sounds of the scene's location (city, park, school, etc.). After the dialogue and sound effects have been edited, the ambient sound can be edited into another audio track to provide sound continuity and realism for the scene. Keep the volume of this track so it remains in the background of the audio portion of the scene, hardly discernable but audible to the viewer. You'll be amazed to hear the difference in a scene with an ambient soundtrack compared with the same scene without it. The former is so much more realistic.

Audio editing is a creative skill that can be used to enhance the effectiveness and impact of the movie on the viewer. Depending on the sophistication of the editing devices used in your program, a single scene can have as many as two to four audio tracks. Before you begin the editing process, make a list of the audio track capability of the editing system and which sound(s) will be edited on which tracks. For example:

Scene	Audio Track	Sound Source
Scene #1 - City	Track 1	Dialogue
	Track 2	Music soundtrack
	Track 3	Ambient street noise
	Track 4	Sound effects: police siren
Scene #2 - Apartment	Track 1	Dialogue
	Track 2	None
	Track 3	Ambient noise (TV/radio)
	Track 4	Sound effects (phone ring)

Throughout this movie, Audio Track 1 will be used for dialogue, Track 2 for music soundtracks, Track 3 for ambient sound, and Track 4 for the insertion of sound effects. Not all tracks will be used for all sounds, but all audio tracks will be consistent throughout the movie.

Graphics and Titles

Opening titles and graphics for your video movie should be designed as part of the storyboarding process of the overall movie. Decisions about the opening and ending graphics need to be made early in the planning process, not during the postproduction stage. Some considerations should include the following:

1. *Content.* What graphic titles will be included? In the opening graphics, will you include just the title of the movie or maybe "produced by _____" as well? Write down which graphics you'll include as part of the opening titles.

2. *Style.* How will the graphics look and how will they appear on the screen? What fonts and colors will be used? Will any special effects or extra equipment (e.g., computers) be needed to produce the graphics? Some movies simply begin with a title screen. Others have included the titles as part of the opening sequence of the movie, keying the titles over the video footage. Which transitions will be used? These are all things the producer/director and the graphics artist can decide on before completing the graphics for the movie (Figure 8.14).

3. *Credits.* What acknowledgments will be listed during the program's opening sequence and final credits? The final credits are important because many students will use the movie as part of their resume or portfolio for college or production programs. Ending credits should list all actors and technicians who worked on the production. Actors are usually listed first, followed by production personnel. Create a list and carefully check cast and crew for placement and spelling of their names. Also, don't forget to thank all of the people who have helped you in your project in the credits. Most student crews will need to borrow props, wardrobes, locations, and equipment to

complete their movie. Most businesses will appreciate a copy of your program and their name listed in the ending credits as a token "thanks" and will be much more receptive to future requests.

Fig. 8.14. An example of title graphics.

Trying to create opening titles and ending credits on the spot during postproduction is likely to take longer and create more mistakes. Preplanning your opening titles and creating a credit list during production is advantageous. If the graphics are planned at the beginning of production, the graphic artist can even design and produce the graphics so they will be ready when postproduction is begun. Many editing systems will create and store graphics for later use in the production process. This is an activity that can be assigned and completed while production on location is being done.

Opening Night: Screening Your Video

Completion of a "minimovie" is a great accomplishment and should be celebrated. Plan a big screening party. Obtain the use of a video projector, a big screen, and an amplified sound system to create a theater atmosphere in a television studio, classroom, or school auditorium. Serve popcorn and sodas, and make sure to invite everyone who took part in the production. You may even want to print programs. Many times, the editor and directors are the only team members present when the project is completed. Other team members and actors have to stop by and watch the finished project on a small monitor in the studio. A big premiere party brings all of the team members together and lets everyone know how important their work on the project really is.

Conclusion

Whether for course content, contests, school presentations, or personal enrichment, the production of a video movie offers an excellent educational opportunity. Students in the television production program get to use their skills in project planning, videography, audio recording, and editing. Language arts skills are used in writing and scripting the story. Visual art students can assist in storyboarding and set design. Theater students can perfect their talents as actors and performers on camera—a task different from performing on stage for a live audience. Finally, all team members benefit from learning the value of teamwork, cooperation, and working together to accomplish long-range goals. In the production of a video movie, students can display advanced skills in an entertaining and accessible format—and have fun, too!

Review Questions

1. What is the difference between complexity and continuity as these terms relate to video movies?

2. What is a treatment?

3. What is an establishing shot, and how is it used in a movie?

4. What is brainstorming, and how does it relate to creating a movie?

5. What is a storyboard? Be sure to list and describe the three components of a story board.

6. What is a cutaway? How is it used in postproduction?

7. List two possible cutaways for each of these scenes:
    A laboratory experiment in a classroom gone bad.

    A zookeeper trying to catch an escaped tiger.

    An FBI agent chasing a suspect through a city park.

8. List and describe five major factors a filmmaker must consider when planning a production.

9. Write three lines of script for this scene. Be sure to include character names, one screen direction, and one camera angle.

    Scene: Two boys trying to remember their locker combination.

10. What is ambient or wild sound? How is it used in movie production?

11. What is a prop? Describe one way to ensure that all props are ready when it is time for scene to be videotaped.

12. List one sound effect that could be used for each of these scenes:

    A Mardi Gras parade _____

    A lunch meeting in a restaurant _____

    A boring lecture in a classroom _____

    Students walking to class in a hallway _____

    A boat race on a lake _____

13. List and describe three aspects to consider when planning graphics for a movie.

14. List and describe three factors you should consider when going to shoot at a location.

15. Write a treatment for a movie idea.

    List and describe two characters that would appear in your movie.

    List four props you would need for your movie.

    List and describe two locations you would use in your movie.

Student Project Plan: Making a Movie!

Objective

To develop students skills in planning, writing, and producing movies.

Name(s) _____   _____

_____   _____

_____   _____

_____   _____

Brainstorming the Idea

List three possible movie "ideas"

1. _____

2. _____

3. _____

Treatment

A treatment is a brief description (three to five sentences) that describes what will happen in the movie. Write a treatment for one of your movie ideas.

Characters

Characters are the main people that will appear in the movie. Make a list of characters that will appear in Scene 1 of your movie idea. Briefly describe each.

Example: John, a young man about age 17, dissatisfied with his job.

1. _____

2. _____

3. _____

4. _____

Script

The script, or dialogue, is what the characters will say in the movie.   Scripts can also indicate camera angles and production ideas to use in the storyboard to create the movie. Write a script for Scene 1 in your movie. Be sure to include stage directions as well as camera instructions. Attach it to this Project Plan when completed.

Storyboards

Storyboards are an essential part of converting a script into a movie. Complete a set of storyboards (see Figures 8.3 and 8.4) for Scene 1. Attach it to this Project Plan when completed.

Props

Props are items (clothes, objects, set decorations) that are needed to make your movie scene realistic. Make a list of props that are needed for Scene 1. Use the Wardrobe and Prop List (see Figure 8.7) and attach it to this Project Plan.

Equipment

Think about all the equipment you will need to record Scene 1 of your movie idea. Complete an Equipment Checklist (see Figure 8.6) for the equipment you will need to record Scene 1 of your movie.

Locations

Places where your movie scenes are recorded are called locations. Make a list of locations that are needed to record Scene 1 of your movie idea. Include a brief description of each.

Example: City Park—People seated on benches, park visitors walking by.

1. _____

2. _____

3. _____

Production

Production involves the actual recording of the movie scenes. Record Scene 1 of your movie idea. Production can occur on location, or you can build sets and record in the television studio.

Postproduction

Editing the raw footage into a finished project. Edit Scene 1 of your movie. Be sure to include opening titles and soundtracks, as well as dialogue, sound effects (if needed), music score (if needed).

Evaluation Sheet: Making a Movie

Name(s) _____

_____

_____

_____

_____

Movie Ideas

Originality . . . .(5 points) _____

Teacher Comments:

Creativity . . . . (5 points) _____

Total Points . . . . (10 points) _____

Treatment

Concept . . . . (5 points) _____

Teacher Comments:

Story development . . . . (5 points) _____

Total Points . . . . (10 points) _____

Character List

Complete Listing . . . . (5 points) _____

Teacher Comments:

Descriptions . . . . (5 points) _____

Total Points . . . . (10 points) _____

Script

Characterization (10 points) _____

Teacher Comments:

Stage directions. . . . .(10 points) _____
Camera angles. . . . .(10 points) _____
Total Points. . . . .(30 points) _____

Storyboards

Drawings. . . . .(10 points) _____

Teacher Comments:

Camera angles. . . . .(10 points) _____
Timings. . . . .(10 points) _____
Total Points. . . . .(30 points) _____

Prop List

Accurate listing/form . . . .(5 points) _____
Creativity . . . .(5 points) _____
Total Points. . . . .(10 points) _____

Equipment List

Accurate listing/form . . . .(5 points) _____

Teacher Comments:

Thorough . . . .(5 points) _____
Total Points` . . . .(10 points) _____

Location Listing

Reflects scene action. . . . .(5 points) _____

Teacher Comments:

Feasible. . . . .(5 points) _____
Total Points. . . . .(10 points) _____

Production

Videography . . . .(15 points) _____

Teacher Comments:

Sound . . . .(15 points) _____

Job performance . . . .(10 points) _____

Total Points. . . . .**(40 points)** _____

Postproduction

Editing techniques . . . .(15 points) _____

Teacher Comments:

Sound editing . . . .(15 points) _____

Titles/graphics. . . . .(10 points) _____

Total Points. . . . .**(40 points)** _____

Total Points Awarded . . . .**(Out of 200)** _____

Teacher Comments:

GLOSSARY

adapter A device used to achieve compatibility between two items of audio/video equipment.

aperture The opening of the camera lens, as controlled by the iris.

audio The sound portion of television production.

audio dub An editing technique that involves erasing the existing audio track on a videotape and replacing it with a new one.

audio mixer An electronic component that facilitates the selection and combination of audio signals.

audio/video mixer A single electronic component that consists of an audio mixer and a video mixer. Also called an A/V mixer.

automatic focus A feature on most camcorders that automatically makes minor focal-length adjustments, thus freeing the videographer from focusing concerns.

automatic gain control A feature on most video cameras and camcorders that, when engaged, boosts the video signal to its optimum output level.

automatic iris A feature on most video cameras and camcorders that automatically adjusts the lens aperture to allow the optimum amount of light to reach the imaging device.

A/V mixer *See* **audio/video mixer.**

BNC A video connector characterized by a single shaft enclosed by a twist-lock mechanism.

backlight A light used in production that is positioned behind the talent and designed to eliminate shadows on background sets and curtains cast by the key light.

balance A potentiometer that lets the technician send each input to either the right or left channel on a stereo audio mixer. Also referred to as "pan."

bank A pair of buses, as on a video mixer.

blocking Planned movements and actions of talent and crew.

bust shot A video shot of a person including the head and shoulders area.

buy-out music Production music purchased for a one-time fee, as opposed to a lease or per-use fee schedule. *See also* **production music.**

camcorder An item of video equipment that uses a video camera permanently attached to a video deck to create and record video signal.

cardioid Another name for the unidirectional microphone pickup pattern. The name "cardioid" comes from the heart shape of the pickup pattern. The terms "super-cardioid," "hyper-cardioid," and "ultra-cardioid" describe more narrow pickup patterns.

CCD *See* **charge-coupled device.**

character generator A video component that allows the typing of words and simple graphics onto the television screen.

charge-coupled device (CCD) An imaging device used in most video cameras and camcorders.

chroma key A video-mixer-based electronic effect, in which a second video source is substituted for a color (or range of shades within a color) within a video shot. For example, a weather reporter stands in front of a green screen. A weather map (the second video source) replaces the green background using the chroma key effect.

clips bin A section of the nonlinear editing system display screen that contains icons representing each audio, video, and graphic element available for use in the video project.

close-up A video shot of a person that includes only the head and neck.

complexity The use of a variety of camera angles and editing to enhance the intensity of action in a scene.

condenser microphone A microphone that contains an element made of two small vibrating magnetized plates.

continuity Preserving the visual coherence and perceived reality of an event.

contrast ratio The comparison of the brightest part of the screen to the darkest part of the screen, expressed as a ratio. The maximum contrast ratio for television production is 30:1.

crawl Graphics that move across the bottom of the television screen, usually from right to left. The weather alert that moves along the bottom of the TV screen is a crawl.

cue (noun) An audio mixer function that allows the user to hear an audio source (usually through headphones) without selecting that source for broadcast or recording; the audio counterpart of a preview monitor.

cue (verb) The act of rewinding or fast-forwarding a video- or audiotape so that the desired section is ready for play.

cut One video shot appearing immediately after the previous one, with no apparent transition.

cutaway shot A video shot used to intercut between two shots in order to avoid jump cuts and continuity problems.

cyclorama (cyc) A large, seamless cloth or curtain that is hung on tracks to provide background for studio sets.

digital editing *See* **nonlinear digital video editing.**

digital zoom A feature found on some camcorders that electronically increases the lens zoom capability by selecting the center of the image and enlarging it digitally.

dimmer switch A control used to gradually increase and decrease the electricity sent to a lighting fixture, thereby affecting the amount of light it emits.

directionality *See* **microphone directionality.**

dissolve A video transition in which the first video signal is gradually replaced by a second video signal.

distribution amplifier An electronic device that boosts the strength of audio, video, or RF (radio frequency) signal and facilitates disbursal of the signal to several outputs.

dolly (noun) A set of casters attached to the legs of a tripod to allow the tripod to roll.

dolly (verb) A forward-backward rolling movement of the camera on top of the tripod dolly.

DV8mm A digital videotape format that consists of magnetic tape 8 millimeters wide in a small plastic videocassette shell. DV8mm is superior in quality to both 8mm and Hi-8.

DVD-R A recordable digital video disc. A DVD-R may be recorded only once and is not a reusable medium. A DVD-R will hold 4.7 gigabytes of data, or enough for approximately 2 hours of video (with audio) recorded in the MPEG2 mode.

DVD-RAM A recordable digital video disc. A DVD-RAM may be recorded, erased, and reused. Like a DVD-R, a DVD-RAM will hold 4.7 gigabytes of data, or enough for approximately 2 hours of video (with audio) recorded in the MPEG2 mode.

dynamic microphone A microphone that contains an element consisting of a diaphragm and moving coil.

editing The process of combining, adding, and deleting audio and video elements to create a television program.

8mm (eight millimeter) A videotape format that consists of magnetic tape 8 millimeters wide in a small plastic videocassette shell. *See also* **Hi-8**.

electronic image stabilization (EIS) A camcorder feature that corrects shaky video shots. When EIS is activated, the camcorder examines each frame of video, compares it with the previous frame, and makes small corrections to standardize the framing of the shot.

element *See* **microphone element.**

establishing shot Video shot used early in the sequence to identify the setting for the following action. Establishes time and location of the scene for the audience.

exporting Recording a finished video program onto a medium such as videotape, DVD, or computer file.

extreme close-up A video shot that includes only part of a person's face.

f-connector A video connector characterized by a single metal wire. F-connectors may be either push-on or screw-post.

fade A video technique in which the picture is gradually replaced with a background color.

fader A vertical slide controller on audio and video equipment.

fader bar *See* **fader.**

fill light A third light used in studio production designed to fill in and eliminate shadow areas caused by the use of a key light.

Firewire Apple computer's registered name for IEEE-1394 digital cable and connectors. *See also* **IEEE-1394.**

flats Wooden frames containing fabrics or lightweight materials used as backgrounds for studio sets.

flying head A video head that engages when the video deck is on "pause," providing a clear still-frame image.

focus Adjustment made to the focal length of the lens to create a sharper, more defined picture.

font A style of type. Many character generators offer the user a menu of several fonts.

frame A complete video picture. NTSC televisions (as used in North America, Japan, and many other countries) display 30 frames each second. Other standards (most notably PAL and SECAM) display 25 frames each second.

frequency response The characteristic of audio equipment that describes the lowest and highest frequencies (pitches) that the equipment can receive, record, and play back. For example, a microphone might have a frequency response of 22 to 18,000 Hz. (Human hearing has a frequency range of 20–20,000 Hz.)

gain An increase in the output of audio or video signal.

gels (gelatins) Colored squares of plastic material used on the front of lights to provide colored lighting on backgrounds and sets.

head A magnet used to record or play a signal on a magnetic medium such as videotape.

head, tripod. *See* **tripod head.**

headroom The space between the top of a person's head and the top of the video screen.

Hi-8 A videotape format that consists of magnetic tape eight millimeters wide in a small plastic videocassette shell. Hi-8 offers a higher-quality image than standard 8mm.

high-speed shutter A camcorder that allows detail enhancement of fast-moving objects by electronically dividing the charge-coupled device into imaging sections.

IEEE-1394 A connecting device used to connect digital video camcorders to personal computers and nonlinear digital editing systems. The IEEE-1394 signal carries audio and video tracks and is capable of speeds up to 400 megabytes per seconds. (IEEE is the Institute of Electrical and Electronic Engineers, a technical/professional society.) *See also* **FireWire and I-Link.**

I-Link Sony's registered name for IEEE-1394 digital cable and connectors. *See also* **IEEE-1394.**

imaging device The part of the video camera or camcorder that converts light into electrical signal.

impedance A resistance to signal flow. Microphones and audio mixers are rated for impedance and can be categorized as high impedance or low impedance.

import , importing The process of recording audio and video segments onto a hard drive (or other storage medium) for use in nonlinear digital video editing.

iris The mechanism that controls the lens aperture.

jack A receptacle for insertion of audio or video cable on audio or video equipment. For example, headphones plug into the audio mixer's headphone jack.

jog Frame-by-frame advancement of a videotape in a VCR or video deck.

jog and shuttle wheel A dial on many video decks and VCRs that controls jog and shuttle functions.

jump cut An awkward shift in continuity when two scenes are abruptly linked through either videotaping or editing

key A function on a video mixer that enables graphics or other video elements to be superimposed on video or colored backgrounds.

key light The main source of illumination in a video production, usually facing the on-camera talent.

lavaliere microphone A small condenser microphone used in television production.

leadroom The area between a subject shot in profile and the edge of the screen that he or she is facing.

lens The curved glass on a video camera or camcorder that collects light.

line-out monitor A monitor that is connected to a recording device to show how the finished product will appear or sound. A line-out monitor may be a video monitor (video product), an audio speaker (audio product), or a television (both audio and video).

logic control an operational feature on higher-quality audiocassette players and recorders in which the tape functions (play, fast-forward, rewind, etc.) are achieved electronically rather than mechanically. Logic controls eliminate the "clunk" sound associated with operation of an audiocassette player or recorder and reduce the wear and tear on the equipment.

long shot A video shot consisting of the entire subject you are shooting.

loop A brief, repeatable audio segment (usually one or two measures long) used as a building block of a song created using music-creation software. Such a song might include a drum loop, a bass loop, a keyboard loop, and a guitar loop, all of which are combined and repeated to create a song.

lux A measurement of light. Lux is used in television production to determine the minimum amount of light (lux rating) needed for camera operation. Hence, a 2-lux camcorder requires less light than a 4-lux camcorder.

macro lens A lens used for videography when the camera-to-object distance is less than 2 feet. The macro lens is usually installed within the zoom lens of the video camera or camcorder.

medium shot A video shot of a person that includes the body from the knee area up.

microphone An audio component that converts sound waves into electrical energy.

microphone directionality The property of a microphone that describes the area from which the microphone collects sound.

microphone element The part of the microphone the converts sound waves into electrical energy.

minidisc A digital audio format characterized by a small, optically recorded disc housed within a 2.5-inch square plastic shell. A minidisc can store 74 to 80 minutes of digital quality audio.

MiniDV A digital videotape format that consists of quarter-inch-wide magnetic tape in a small plastic videocassette shell.

minitripod A small, three-legged mounting device used to hold 35mm cameras, digital cameras, and small camcorders. Minitripods are about six inches tall and are usually used on a tabletop.

modulator *See* **RF modulator.**

monitor, audio A speaker or headphone set.

monitor, video A video screen. A video monitor accepts video signal and does not have a tuner.

monochrome A video picture consisting of different saturations of a single color, usually gray. The technical term for black-and-white television.

monopod A one-legged mounting device used to help the videographer steady a handheld camera shot and reduce fatigue.

MP3 (MPEG-1 Audio Layer-3) A digital audio format for compressing sound into a very small computer file, while preserving the original level of quality. MP3 uses an algorithm to achieve this compression, reducing data about sound that is not within the normal range of human hearing. (MPEG is the Motion Picture Experts Group.)

nonlinear digital video editing Postproduction work using audio and video elements saved as digital files on a computer hard drive or other storage device. Nonlinear digital video editing is characterized by the ability to work on segments in any sequence (as opposed to traditional linear editing, which requires working from the beginning of the production until the end).

nonlinear editing *See* **nonlinear digital video editing.**

nonlinear editing system A computer system that performs nonlinear digital video editing functions.

omnidirectional A microphone pickup pattern in which the microphone "hears" equally well from all sides.

one-eighth-inch mini A small audio connector used frequently in consumer electronics.

one-quarter-inch phone A connector used in audio production that is characterized by its single shaft with locking tip.

on-screen display A function on many VCRs and televisions in which operational functions (tint, brightness, VCR function, programming, etc.) are displayed graphically on the television screen.

optical zoom lens A camcorder lens with a variable focal length. The optical zoom lens achieves this variability by moving a series of glass lenses inside a larger lens housing.

over-the-shoulder shot A video shot that places the back of the head and shoulder of a person (e.g., an interviewer) in the foreground and the subject of the shot in the background.

pan A horizontal movement of a camera on top of a tripod.

pan *See* **balance.**

phantom power Electricity provided by audio mixers for use by condenser microphones connected to the audio mixer. Some microphones require phantom power and must be connected to audio mixers that provide it.

phono (RCA) A connector used in audio and video components that is characterized by its single connection post and metal flanges.

pickup pattern The description of the directionality of a microphone. The two dominant microphone pickup patterns are omnidirectional and unidirectional.

pixel A single section of a charge-coupled device capable of distinguishing chromanance (color) and luminance (brightness); professional slang for "picture element."

postproduction The phase of television production that includes all activity after the raw footage is shot.

pot *See* **potentiometer.**

potentiometer (pot) An audio mixer level control in the form of a dial that moves clockwise (toward the right) and counterclockwise (toward the left). Moving the pot clockwise increases the level, and moving the pot counterclockwise decreases the level.

pressure zone microphone (PZM) A microphone consisting of a metal plate and a small microphone element. The PZM collects and processes all sound waves that strike the metal plate.

preview monitor A video monitor that displays the picture from a video source. The technical director uses the preview monitor to evaluate a video source before selecting it.

production music Musical selections created specifically for use in audio and video programs. When customers buy production music, they also buy copyright permissions not granted with standard music purchases, thus averting copyright violations.

props Objects used in the scene either by actors or as part of the set design.

quick release A system for mounting a camcorder on a tripod. A quick release system provides a metal or plastic plate that is attached to the bottom of the camcorder. That plate easily attaches and locks into the tripod head.

RCA connector *See* **phono (RCA).**

record review A feature on many camcorders that allows the videographer to see the last few seconds of video recorded on the videotape.

rendering The process by which the nonlinear editing system (the computer) actually creates each transition, effect, or graphic.

resolution The sharpness of the picture. Resolution can be measured numerically by establishing the number of scanning lines used to create each frame of video.

RF modulator An electronic device that converts audio or video signal into RF (radio frequency) signal.

RF signal Modulated composite (video and audio) signal produced by television stations and VCRs and processed by televisions.

RF splitter A device that multiplies an RF signal. A person could use an RF splitter to send the signal from one VCR to two or more televisions.

Rule of Thirds The videography concept that states that the subject, or most interesting part of a video shot, should be located along the "thirds"—one-third and two-thirds—both vertically and horizontally.

S-VHS A video format that uses VHS-sized cassettes and half-inch S-VHS tape and produces a signal with more than 400 lines of resolution. S-VHS signal cannot be recorded on a VHS tape or recorded or played on a VHS VCR.

S-VHS-C A video format using S-VHS videotape in a compact shell (*see* **VHS-C**). S-VHS-C records an S-VHS quality signal. The tape can be played in an S-VHS VCR using an adapter.

scrim A fiber or plastic covering placed on the front of a lighting fixture to diffuse (spread out) the light.

scroll Graphics that roll from the bottom to the top of the screen (e.g., end credits).

send A secondary output on an audio mixer.

shotgun microphone A microphone with an extremely directional pickup pattern.

shuttle A variable-rate search, forward or reverse, of a videotape using a VCR capable of such an operation.

signal-to-noise ratio A numerical value, expressed in decibels (dB), that represents the strength of a video signal compared with the amount of video noise present.

slate A small blackboard-like device recorded on camera that gives program information (name, title, date, take numbers).

sound bite A videotaped segment in which the audio and video portions of the tape must remain in sync. Sound bites are usually three to five seconds in length.

spotmeter A device that measures the intensity of reflected light, as on a lighted set.

stand-up An on-camera shot of a reporter as he or she presents information about the topic.

storyboarding The process of planning a video project that includes drawing a simple sketch of the desired shot, planning the accompanying audio, and estimating the duration of each element.

studio address system An intercom system that allows communication between control-room personnel and personnel working on the studio floor.

surface mount microphone A microphone that is flat on one side, has no handle, and lies flat on a tabletop or other surface. Surface mount microphones are designed to be used in group discussions, workshops, and other situations in which subjects are seated around a table.

surge protector An electronic device that protects electronic equipment from power fluctuations.

tag A standard format for the final sentence of script ending an ENG report. Identifies the reporter (name) and station affiliation.

teleprompter An electronic version of cue cards; the talent's script is displayed and manipulated on a computer monitor or refracted through a glass and mirror in front of the camera lens.

television A combination tuner, RF (radio frequency) modulator, picture tube, and audio speaker that converts RF signal into picture and sound.

tilt A vertical movement of a video camera or camcorder on top of a tripod.

time-base corrector (TBC) A video component that digitizes inherently unstable analog video signal and converts it into rock-solid video. A TBC usually has controls for manipulating the output signal's color, brightness, and strength. The advent of digital video has reduced the need for time-base correction.

tracking The video control that allows proper placement of the videotape across the video and audio heads.

treatment A brief description of a film topic or idea.

trim (audio) An audio mixer control (usually a potentiometer) that lets the audio technician adjust each individual microphone so that all microphones will perform at the same level. Also referred to as "gain."

trim (editing) The editing technique of eliminating part of the beginning or end of a video or audio clip used in the nonlinear digital video editing process. Trimming a clip allows the editor to select the exact point where the imported clip will begin and end.

tripod A three-legged mounting device for a video camera or camcorder that provides stability.

tripod dolly A combination tripod and dolly.

tripod head The top-most part of a tripod. The tripod head provides the mechanism for mounting the camcorder on the tripod and facilitates panning and tilting motions.

truck A lateral movement of the camera achieved by moving or rolling the tripod dolly to the left ("truck left") or right ("truck right").

tuner An element of a television set that allows the user to select specific signals and frequencies (channels) to be shown on the picture tube and played through the speaker.

unidirectional A microphone pickup pattern in which the microphone processes most of its signal from sound collected in front of the microphone and very little from the sides and back.

VHS A videocassette format characterized by a plastic shell and half-inch-wide videotape. VHS is an abbreviation for "video home system," created by the JVC company. VHS is the dominant videotape format for home VCRs and videotaped programs and blank cassettes.

VHS-C A videocassette format characterized by a plastic shell and half-inch-wide videotape. VHS-C-recorded tape is compatible with VHS if an adapter is used. VHS-C was developed as a way to create VHS signal with a smaller videocassette, and thus a smaller camcorder.

video The visual portion of television production.

video camera A video component consisting of a lens, a viewfinder, and at least one imaging device that converts light into electrical video signal.

video deck An electronic component used for recording and playback of videotape. It consists of a video/audio head assembly, a mechanism for transporting videotape past the heads, and operational controls.

video mixer A video component that allows the selection of a video source from several source inputs. Most video mixers allow the technician to perform wipes, dissolves, and fades.

video noise A poor-quality video signal within the standard video signal. Also known as "snow."

video signal The electrical signal produced by video components.

videocassette A length of videotape wound around two reels and enclosed in a plastic shell.

videocassette recorder (VCR) An electronic component consisting of a tuner, an RF (radio frequency) modulator, and a video deck used for recording and playback of a videocassette.

videographer A person who operates a video camera or camcorder.

videography Operation of a video camera or camcorder in video production.

videography repertoire A collection of six video shots that represents the standard work of videography. All videographers should learn to properly compose the shots in the videography repertoire.

videotape A thin strip of plastic material containing metal particles capable of recording and storing a magnetic charge.

viewfinder or viewscreen A small video monitor mounted on a video camera or camcorder that provides a view of the video image to the videographer. Viewfinders or viewscreens may be presented as eye-pieces, as small screens mounted on the side of the camcorder, or as larger video monitors mounted near the top of a studio camera.

volume unit (VU) meter A device used to measure the intensity of an audio signal.

white balance The process of adjusting the video camera or camcorder's color response to the surrounding light.

wild sound Random sounds recorded on location to add to the soundtrack to add ambience and realism.

windscreen A form-fitting foam cover for the top of the microphone that eliminates the rumbling sound caused by wind and sudden bursts of air.

wipe A video transition in which one video source replaces another with a distinct line or lines of definition.

wireless microphone system A microphone system consisting of a microphone, an FM transmitter, and a tuned receiving station that eliminates the need for long runs of microphone cable.

XLR An audio connector characterized by three prongs covered by a metal sheath.

zoom lens A lens with a variable focal length.

INDEX

189

FIGURE CREDITS

All figures © 2004 Keith Kyker and Christopher Curchy, unless noted.

Chapter 1

Figure 1.3: Special thanks to Mary Jane Ross

Chapter 3

Figures 3.1–3.4, 3.7, 3.8: Image courtesy Behringer USA (www.behringer.com)

Figure 3.14: Image courtesy of Davenport Music Library (www.davenportmusic.com)

Figure 3.15: Photo courtesy of Sony Pictures Digital, Inc.

Figure 3.16: Graphic courtesy of SmartSound Software (www.smartsound.com) (800) 454-1900, SmartSound Software, Inc., 8550 Balboa Blvd., Suite 180, Northridge, CA 91325

Chapter 4

Figure 4.7: Photograph compliments of MacroSystem Digital Video (www.casablanca.tv)

Chapter 6

Figures 6.2–6.8, 6.12: Photograph compliments of MacroSystem Digital Video (www.casablanca.tv)

Figure 6.6: Photo courtesy of Sony Pictures Digital, Inc.

Figures 6.9, 6.10, 6.11: Source images copyright © 1997 The Learning Company, Inc. and its licensors

Chapter 7

Figure 7.7: VT[3] Image copyright c2004 Newtek, Inc. Used with permission.

Figure 7.16: Photo courtesy of LightTech (www.lighttech.com)

Figure 7.19: Photo courtesy of Extech Instruments Corp. www.extech.com

Chapter 8

Figure 8.14: Photograph compliments of MacroSystem Digital Video (www.casablanca.tv)

ABOUT THE AUTHORS

KEITH KYKER is Educational Media Specialist, Addie R. Lewis Middle School, Valparaiso, Florida. Before becoming a media specialist, he taught television production, media production, public speaking, and English at the high school and college levels. He was named Teacher of the Year for Okaloosa County, FL for 1999-2000, and served on the committee that developed the assessment for National Board Certification for library media.

CHRISTOPHER CURCHY is Educational Media Specialist, North Lake Park Community School, Orlando, FL, and Adjunct Professor, University of Central Florida Educational Technologies Graduate Program. With Keith Kyker, Curchy is the co-author of 9 educational technology books for Libraries Unlimited. They have presented at 50 conferences nationwide, host the popular Web site www.schooltv.com, and write the syndicated column "Video Viewfinder" for *Florida Media Quarterly*.

CPSIA information can be obtained
at www.ICGtesting.com
Printed in the USA
FFOW01n1938230615
14549FF